# THE CONTENTS

OF THE

# FIFTH AND SIXTH BOOKS OF EUCLID.

London: C. J. CLAY AND SONS,
CAMBRIDGE UNIVERSITY PRESS WAREHOUSE,
AVE MARIA LANE.
Glasgow: 50, WELLINGTON STREET.

Leipzig: F. A. BROCKHAUS.
New York: THE MACMILLAN COMPANY.
Bombay: E. SEYMOUR HALE.

# THE CONTENTS

OF THE

# FIFTH AND SIXTH BOOKS OF EUCLID

*ARRANGED AND EXPLAINED*

BY

M. J. M. HILL, M.A., D.Sc., F.R.S.

PROFESSOR OF MATHEMATICS AT UNIVERSITY COLLEGE, LONDON;
LATE EXAMINER IN THE UNIVERSITY OF LONDON,
AND FOR THE CIVIL SERVICE OF INDIA.

CAMBRIDGE:
AT THE UNIVERSITY PRESS.
1900

Cambridge:
PRINTED BY J. AND C. F. CLAY,
AT THE UNIVERSITY PRESS.

# PREFACE.

THE object of this work is to remove the chief difficulties felt by those who desire to understand the Sixth Book of Euclid. It contains nothing beyond the capacity of those who have mastered the first four Books, and has been prepared for their use. It is the result of an experience of teaching the subject extending over nearly twenty years. The arrangement here adopted has been used by the Author in teaching for the past three years and has been more readily understood than the methods in ordinary use, which he had previously employed.

The Sixth Book depends to a very large extent on the Fifth, but this Fifth Book is so difficult that it is usually entirely omitted with the exception of the Fifth Definition, which is retained not for the purpose of proving all the properties of ratio required in the Sixth Book, but only for demonstrating two important propositions, viz., the 1st and 33rd.

The other properties of ratio required in the Sixth Book are usually assumed, or so-called algebraic demonstrations are supplied. The employment side by side of these two methods of dealing with ratio confuses the learner, because, not being equivalent, they do not constitute, when used in this way, a firm basis for the train of reasoning which he is attempting to follow. A better method is sometimes attempted. This is to insist on the mastering of the Fifth Book, expressed in modern form as in the Syllabus of the Association for the Improvement of Geometrical Teaching, before commencing the Sixth Book.

But it is far too difficult for all but the best pupils, and even they do not grasp the train of reasoning as a whole, though they readily admit the truth of the propositions singly as consequences of the fundamental definitions, which are

(I) The fifth definition, which is the test for the sameness of two ratios.

(II) The seventh definition, which is the test for distinguishing the greater of two unequal ratios from the smaller.

*(III) The tenth definition, which defines "Duplicate Ratio."

*(IV) The definition marked A by Simson, which defines the process for compounding ratios.

In order to make things clear, it is necessary to explain what it is that makes Euclid's Fifth Book so very difficult.

There is first the difficulty arising out of Euclid's notation for magnitudes and numbers. This has been entirely removed in most modern editions by using an algebraic notation and need not therefore be further considered.

There is next the difficulty arising out of Euclid's use of the word "ratio," and the idea represented by it.

His definition of ratio furnishes no satisfactory answer to the question, "What is a ratio?" and it is of such a nature that no indication is afforded of the answer to the still more important question, "How is a ratio to be measured?" As Euclid makes no use of the definition in his argument, it is useless to examine it further, but it is worth while to try to get at his view of ratio. He asserts indirectly that a ratio is a magnitude, because in the seventh definition he states the conditions which must be satisfied in order that one ratio may be *greater* than another. Now the word "greater" can only be applied to a magnitude. Hence Euclid must have considered a ratio to be a magnitude†. To this conclusion it may be objected that if Euclid thought that a ratio was a magnitude he would not so constantly have spoken of the *sameness* of two ratios, but of their *equality*. One can only surmise that, whenever it was possible, he desired to leave open all questions as to the nature of ratio, and to present all his propositions as logical deductions from his fundamental definitions. Yet the question as to the nature of ratio is one which forces itself on the careful reader, and is a source of the greatest perplexity, culminating when he reaches the 11th and 13th Propositions.

The 11th Proposition may be stated thus:—

| | |
|---|---|
| If | $A : B$ is the same as $C : D$, |
| and if | $C : D$ is the same as $E : F$, |
| then | $A : B$ is the same as $E : F$. |

* These are not required until the 6th Book is reached.

† Some writers maintain that the word "greater" as applied to ratio, is not used in the same sense as when it is applied to magnitudes. This seems to make matters far more difficult.

Now if a ratio is a magnitude, this only expresses that if $X = Y$, and if $Y = Z$, then $X = Z$.

As this result follows from Euclid's First Axiom it is difficult to see the need for a proof.

This only becomes apparent when the reader realises that Euclid's procedure may be described thus:—

Let $A$, $B$, $C$, $D$ be four magnitudes satisfying the conditions of the Fifth Definition, and let $C$, $D$, $E$, $F$ be four magnitudes also satisfying the same conditions, then it is proved that $A$, $B$, $E$, $F$ also satisfy the conditions of that definition.

Remarks of a somewhat similar nature apply to the 13th Proposition.

In this book it is shewn that two commensurable magnitudes determine a real number; and this real number is called the *measure of their ratio.* The proof of the proposition that two incommensurable magnitudes of the same kind determine a real number (which is taken as the measure of their ratio) is too difficult to find a place in an elementary text-book like this.

A still greater difficulty than the preceding arises from the fact that Euclid furnishes no explanation of the steps by which he reached his fundamental definitions.

To write down a definition, and then draw conclusions from it, is a process which is useful in Advanced Mathematics; but it is wholly unsuitable for elementary teaching. It seems not unlikely that Euclid reached his fundamental definitions as conclusions to elaborate trains of reasoning, but that finding great difficulty in expressing this reasoning in words owing to the absence of an algebraic notation, he preferred to write down his definitions as the basis of his argument, and to present the propositions as logical deductions from his definitions.

Apparently he has left no trace of the steps by which he reached his fundamental definitions; and one of the chief objects of this book is to reconstruct a path which can be followed by beginners from ideas of a simpler order to those on which his work is based.

The most vital of his definitions is the Fifth, on reaching which the beginner, who has read the first four books of Euclid, experiences a sense of discontinuity. He knows nothing which can lead him directly to it, he has no ideas of a simpler order with which to connect it; and he is therefore reduced to learning it by rote.

His teacher may show him that it contains the definition of Proportion given in treatises on Algebra; but even with this assistance it remains difficult for him to remember its details. He may and frequently does learn to apply it correctly in demonstrating the 1st and 33rd Propositions of the Sixth Book, but the Author's experience both of teaching and examining leads him to the belief that it is not really understood.

The explanation here given of the Fifth Definition, apart from the actual notation employed, is that given by De Morgan in his treatise on the Connexion of Number and Magnitude published in the year 1836, and is made clear by a device for exhibiting the order of succession of the multiples of two magnitudes of the same kind, when arranged together in a single series in ascending order of magnitude. This device is called *the relative multiple scale of the two magnitudes.* The notation employed to exhibit it is substantially due to Professor A. E. H. Love, F.R.S. This notation attaches a graphical representation to the Fifth Definition, which appeals to the eye of the learner (See Arts. 29—34).

The seventh definition, as will presently be shewn, is not required.

The tenth definition, which defines Duplicate Ratio, is here based on that marked A by Simson (See Art. 129).

Definition A, which defines the process for Compounding Ratios, is fully explained in four stages, commencing with the general idea on which the process is based, and ending with the proof of the fact that the process employed will always lead to consistent results (See Art. 127).

There remains but one great difficulty for consideration. This is the indirectness of Euclid's line of argument, arising from the fact that he uses the Seventh Definition where the Fifth alone need be employed. His Fifth Definition states the conditions which must be satisfied in order that two ratios may be the same (or if ratios are magnitudes, that they may be equal).

*If this definition is a good and sound one, it is evident that it ought to be possible to deduce from it all the properties of equal ratios. This is in fact the case.* It is wholly unnecessary to employ the Seventh Definition, which refers to unequal ratios, to prove any of the properties of equal ratios. Its use only renders the proofs of the propositions indirect and artificial and consequently difficult. Not only does no inconvenience result from avoiding its use, but it is possible to get rid of the latter part of the 8th Proposition, and of the whole of the 10th and 13th

Propositions, which deal with unequal ratios, and of the 14th, 20th and 21st Propositions of the Fifth Book, which are particular cases of the 16th, 22nd and 23rd Propositions respectively.

The remaining Propositions are demonstrated by means of the Fifth Definition alone; and all, with a single exception, fall under one or other of two well recognised types.

These types correspond to the two forms of the conditions for the sameness of two relative multiple scales (or two ratios). [See Prop. VIII. (i), (ii).]

The first form of the conditions is Euclid's Test for Equal Ratios as stated in the Fifth Definition of the Fifth Book. It is the one which springs most naturally out of the nature of the subject. It contains three classes of alternatives, one of which appears only when the magnitudes of the ratios are commensurable. Sometimes it is possible to examine all three classes of alternatives in the same way. On the other hand, in the extremely important Propositions Euc. V. 16, 22, 23, the examination of the cases in which the ratios are commensurable has to be conducted upon different lines to those which are applicable when they are not commensurable. This it is quite possible to do, but the line of argument is artificial and therefore difficult for a beginner, as will be seen by consulting Notes 6, 9, and 11 at the end of the book. The proofs of Props. 16, 22, 23 as completed by these Notes depend on the use of Prop. 62 (Euc. V. 4), but the way in which that proposition has to be used does not suggest itself naturally.

It is on this account that the second form of the conditions for the sameness of two relative multiple scales (Prop. VIII. (ii)), has been introduced into this book. So far as the Author knows it was first published by Stolz (See Art. 37). It contains four classes of alternatives, but it has this very great advantage over Euclid's form that the examination of all the four classes of alternatives can always be conducted upon the same lines.

Reference has been made above to one Proposition which does not fall under either of the above recognized types. This is Prop. 61 (Euc. V. 24). The proof here given is Euclid's. It is very much shorter than any direct deduction of it from either form of the conditions for the sameness of two scales. At the same time its artificial character stands out in striking contrast to the directness of the proofs of the other propositions.

The plan followed in this work is to explain at an early stage what the relative multiple scale of two magnitudes is, then to prove a few of the simpler properties of relative multiple scales, then to point out that these propositions accord with the ideas of ratio, formed by learners long before they commenced to read Geometry, in so far as those ideas have assumed definite shape. In this way the mind of the reader is led to the idea that two magnitudes of the same kind determine not only a relative multiple scale, but also a ratio; so that he sees why, whenever two relative multiple scales are the same, Euclid expressed that fact in the statement that the ratio of the magnitudes determining the first relative multiple scale is the same as the ratio of the magnitudes determining the second relative multiple scale.

In fact all that Euclid proves in regard to the sameness of two ratios may be conveniently expressed as the proof of the sameness of two relative multiple scales, and the advantage of proceeding in this way is this:—

The argument is made to relate to a thing which is completely defined, viz., the relative multiple scale of two magnitudes; whilst in Euclid's argument it is not made clear what a ratio is; and the lack of information on this point is a serious obstacle to the learner.

The determination of the stage at which the idea of ratio should be introduced into the argument is one of great difficulty. Complex as the idea is, it is formed by every one at an early age. As soon as a child can recognise an object from a drawing of it, he has formed the idea of similar figures, and therefore he is able to see that the ratio of two of the dimensions of the object is the same as that of the corresponding dimensions of the drawing. When however the use of the idea, and its introduction into Algebra and Geometry are under consideration, its complexity becomes apparent. There is no necessity, arising out of the nature of the subject, for introducing the idea of ratio into the statement of any of the Propositions in the Fifth Book, with the possible exception of the 8th, 10th and 13th, which deal with unequal ratios and are not required for the Sixth Book.

It is not until the subject of Compounding Ratios is reached that the introduction of the idea becomes desirable. I believe that it will be ultimately recognised that it is best to postpone its introduction until the stage just mentioned has been reached. At the same time I have not ventured to do this in this book, as I desire to conform to established practice, so far as is possible, consistently with clearness of treatment.

Several alterations have been made in the order of the Propositions. De Morgan pointed out that learners found great difficulty in reading the Fifth Book on account of the abstract character of the reasoning, its application to something concrete not being easily perceived. Accordingly in this work Propositions from the Sixth Book are taken as soon as a sufficient number of Propositions from the Fifth Book have been proved to make it possible to deal logically with those in the Sixth Book.

Further alterations made in the order of the Propositions are due to the desire to indicate at an early stage of the work a line of argument which may be followed in order to reach the idea of ratio.

The principal alteration in the proofs is of course the use of the Theory of Relative Multiple Scales in the Propositions of the Fifth Book, in the 1st and 33rd Propositions of the Sixth Book, and in the proof of the first part of the 2nd Proposition of the Sixth Book, where it has the advantage not only of proving all that Euclid does, but also of giving several other propositions which (if required) must be deduced from Euclid's result by the use of other Propositions in the Fifth Book.

With regard to the enunciations no attempt has been made to adhere to Euclid's words. All those propositions which may be viewed either as expressing properties of equal ratios or of the sameness of certain relative multiple scales are enunciated from both these points of view. In the part of the book which precedes the section on ratio (Arts. 62—70), these propositions are enunciated first as properties of relative multiple scales, and secondly as properties of equal ratios for the sake of reference only, inasmuch as the term "ratio" has not yet been explained. After the section on ratio the order of the two modes of enunciation is inverted, as possibly more convenient for reference.

This work contains demonstrations of all the Propositions of the Fifth Book except Nos. 8, 10, 13, which depend on the Seventh Definition, and which are not used in the Sixth Book; of all the Propositions in the Sixth Book together with those marked *A, B, C* in Simson's Euclid and beside these the following:—

The Proposition here numbered 7 contains the earlier part of Euc. v. 8, and is an extremely useful proposition.

Prop. 8 shows the equivalence of the two forms of the conditions to be satisfied in order that two relative multiple scales (or two ratios) may be the same.

Prop. 11 shows that two commensurable magnitudes have the same relative multiple scale as two whole numbers.

Prop. 12 relates to differing relative multiple scales; and with Props. 9 and 11 is very useful in developing the idea of ratio.

Props. 24, 59, 60 and 63 appear here chiefly but not entirely on account of their bearing on the theory of the point at infinity on a straight line.

Props. 36 and 37 are connected with the Theory of Duplicate Ratio.

Prop. 39 shows that the rectangle contained by the diagonals of a quadrilateral cannot exceed the sum of the rectangles contained by the opposite sides. It includes the Proposition marked D in Simson's edition of the Sixth Book.

There are given in suitable positions in the book, the definitions of Harmonic Points and Lines, of the Pole and Polar, of Inversion, of the Radical Axis and the Centres of Similitude of Two Circles, and (so far as is possible without explaining the use of the Negative Sign in Geometry) of Cross or Anharmonic Ratio, with the sole object of rendering intelligible the terminology employed in a number of interesting examples in the book.

The Author believes that he has not taken without acknowledgment from other text-books anything which is not common property.

His special thanks are due to the Cambridge University Press Syndicate, who have made the publication of the book possible; and to his friend and former pupil, Mr L. N. G. Filon, M.A., for valuable suggestions and assistance whilst the book was passing through the press.

He will be grateful to his readers for suggestions and corrections.

# TABLE OF CONTENTS*.

## SECTION I.



* A list of the abbreviations employed follows the Table of Contents.

## SECTION II.

PROPOSITIONS 9—16. THE SIMPLER PROPOSITIONS IN THE THEORY OF RELATIVE MULTIPLE SCALES (AND THE THEORY OF RATIOS) WITH GEOMETRICAL APPLICATIONS. FIRST SERIES.

PROP. 9. $A : B = nA : nB$, | i.e. $[A, B] \simeq [nA, nB]$.

*Arithmetical Applications:—*

$r : s = nr : ns$ i.e. $[r, s] \simeq [nr, ns]$.

$r : s = \frac{r}{s} : 1$ i.e. $[r, s] \simeq \left[\frac{r}{s}, 1\right]$.

| | | |
|---|---|---|
| 10. If $A : B = C : D$, | i.e. if | $[A, B] \simeq [C, D]$, |
| and if $A : B = E : F$, | and if | $[A, B] \simeq [E, F]$, |
| then $C : D = E : F$. | then | $[C, D] \simeq [E, F]$. |
| 11. $a : b = aN : bN$ | i.e. | $[a, b] \simeq [aN, bN]$. |

12. If $A$, $B$, $C$ are three magnitudes of the same kind, and if $A$ and $B$ are unequal, then $[A, C]$ is not the same as $[B, C]$.

13. If two straight lines be cut by any number of parallel straight lines, then the scale of two segments of one straight line is the same as the scale of the two corresponding segments of the other straight line.

14. Given three segments of straight lines, to find a fourth such that the scale of the first and second segments is the same as that of the third and fourth.

15. To divide a straight line similarly to a given divided straight line.

16. From a given straight line to cut off any part required.

## SECTION III.

A CHAPTER ON RATIO.

## SECTION IV.

PROPOSITIONS 17—24. THE SIMPLER PROPOSITIONS IN THE THEORY OF RELATIVE MULTIPLE SCALES (AND THE THEORY OF RATIOS) WITH GEOMETRICAL APPLICATIONS. SECOND SERIES.

PROP. 17. Parallelograms or triangles having the same altitude are proportional to their bases.

18. In equal circles or in the same circle,

(1) angles at the centres are proportional to the arcs on which they stand.

(2) angles at the circumferences are proportional to the arcs on which they stand.

(3) sectors are proportional (*a*) to their arcs,

(*b*) to their angles.

| | | | | |
|---|---|---|---|---|
| PROP. 19. If | $A : B = C : D$, | i.e. if | $[A, B] \simeq [C, D]$, |
| then | $B : A = D : C$, | then | $[B, A] \simeq [D, C]$. |
| 20. If | | $A = B$, | | |
| then | $A : C = B : C$, | then | $[A, C] \simeq [B, C]$, |
| and | $C : A = C : B$, | and | $[C, A] \simeq [C, B]$. |
| 21. If | $A : C = B : C$, | i.e. if | $[A, C] \simeq [B, C]$, |
| or if | $C : A = C : B$, | or if | $[C, A] \simeq [C, B]$, |
| | then | $A = B$. | | |

22. If $A$, $B$, $C$, $D$ are magnitudes of the same kind, and if

| | | | |
|---|---|---|---|
| | $A : B = C : D$, | | $[A, B] \simeq [C, D]$, |
| then | $A : C = B : D$. | then | $[A, C] \simeq [B, D]$. |

23. If two sides of a triangle are divided proportionally, so that the segments terminating at the vertex common to the two sides correspond to each other, then the straight line joining the points of division is parallel to the other side.

24. (i) A given segment of a straight line can be divided *internally* into segments having the ratio of one given line to another in one way only.

(ii) A given segment of a straight line can be divided *externally* into segments having the ratio of one given line to any other not equal to it in one way only.

## SECTION V.

### PROPOSITIONS 25—32. SIMILAR FIGURES.

PROP. 25. Rectilineal figures which are similar to the same rectilineal figure are similar to one another.

26. If the three angles of one triangle are respectively equal to the three angles of another triangle, then the triangles are similar.

27. If the sides taken in order of one triangle are proportional to the sides taken in order of another triangle, then the triangles are similar.

28. If two sides of one triangle are proportional to two sides of another triangle and the included angles are equal, then the triangles are similar.

29. If two triangles have one angle of the one equal to one angle of the other, and the sides about one other angle in each proportional in such a manner that the sides opposite to the equal angles correspond, then the triangles have their remaining angles either equal or supplementary, and in the former case the triangles are similar.

30. On a given straight line to describe a rectilineal figure similar and similarly situated to a given rectilineal figure.

31. Two similar rectilineal figures may be divided into the same number of triangles such that every triangle in either figure is similar to one triangle in the other figure.

## SECTION VI.

### Propositions 33, 34. Miscellaneous Propositions.



## SECTION VII.

### Propositions 35—37. The Compounding of Ratios:—Duplicate Ratio.

# SECTION VIII.

## PROPOSITIONS 38—49. ON AREAS.

## SECTION IX.

PROPOSITIONS 50—55. MISCELLANEOUS GEOMETRICAL PROPOSITIONS.



## SECTION X.

PROPOSITIONS 56—63. THE REMAINING IMPORTANT THEOREMS IN THE THEORIES OF SCALES AND OF RATIO.

PROP. 60. If $A$, $B$, $C$, $D$ be four harmonic points, $A$ and $C$ being conjugate, and if $O$ be the middle point of $AC$, then $OC$ is a mean proportional between $OB$ and $OD$.

61. If $A : C = X : Z$, and if $B : C = Y : Z$, then $A+B : C = X+Y : Z$. | i.e. if $[A, C] \simeq [X, Z]$, and if $[B, C] \simeq [Y, Z]$, then $[A+B, C] \simeq [X+Y, Z]$.

*Arithmetical Application of the Process of Aggregating Ratio.*

$r : s$ aggregated with $u : v = vr + us : vs$.

(This corresponds to the Arithmetical Theorem $\frac{r}{s} + \frac{u}{v} = \frac{vr+us}{vs}$.)

62. If $A : B = X : Y$, then $rA : sB = rX : sY$. | i.e. if $[A, B] \simeq [X, Y]$, then $[rA, sB] \simeq [rX, sY]$.

63. If $K$, $L$, $M$, $P$ be four straight lines in proportion, if the lengths of $L$ and $M$ be fixed, if the length of $K$ can be made smaller than that of any line however small, to show that the length of $P$ can be made greater than that of any line $Q$, however great $Q$ may be.

## SECTION XI.

Propositions 64, 65. Other Propositions in the Theory of Ratio.

PROP. 64. If $A$, $B$, $C$, $D$ are magnitudes of the same kind, and if $A : B = C : D$, then

$$A \sim C : B \sim D = A : B.$$

65. If $A$, $B$, $C$, $D$ are magnitudes of the same kind, and if $A : B = C : D$, then the sum of the greatest and least of the four magnitudes is greater than that of the other two.

Propositions in the Notes.

PROP. 66. $$\frac{rA}{s} = r\left(\frac{A}{s}\right).$$

67. $$[A, B] \simeq \left[\frac{rA}{n}, \frac{rB}{n}\right].$$

## LIST OF ABBREVIATIONS.

| | |
|---|---|
| $+$ | Plus. |
| $-$ | Minus. |
| $=$ | Equal to. |
| $<$ | Less than. |
| $>$ | Greater than. |
| $A \sim B$ | The difference of $A$ and $B$. |
| $A : B$ | The ratio of $A$ to $B$. |
| $A : B :: C : D$ | The ratio of $A$ to $B$ is the same as the ratio of $C$ to $D$. |
| $[A, B]$ | The relative multiple scale of $A$, $B$. (Art. 33.) |
| $\simeq$ | Is the same as. (Art. 33.) |
| $[A, B] \simeq [C, D]$ | The relative multiple scale of $A$, $B$ is the same as the relative multiple scale of $C$, $D$. (Art. 33.) |
| $\divideontimes$ | Compounded with. (Art. 179.) |
| $\frown$ | Aggregated with. (Art. 191.) |

# SECTION I.

PROPOSITIONS 1—8.

ON MAGNITUDES AND THEIR MULTIPLES.

### Art. 1. Number.

In this book except where otherwise stated the word Number will be used as an abbreviation for Positive Whole Number.

### Notation for Number.

A Number will always be denoted by a *small* letter.

### Art. 2. Notation for Magnitude.

A Magnitude will be denoted throughout this book by a *capital* letter*.

### Art. 3. *Def.* 1. MULTIPLE.

**One magnitude is said to be a multiple of another magnitude, when the former contains the latter an exact number of times.**

*e.g.* (1) If $A = 5B$,

then $A$ is a multiple of $B$,

or, more particularly, $A$ is the fifth multiple of $B$.

(2) If $A = rB$,

then $A$ is a multiple of $B$,

or, more particularly, $A$ is the $r$th multiple of $B$.

It will be in agreement with the above nomenclature, when $A$ is equal to $B$, to say that $A$ is the first multiple of $B$; and to call the $r$th multiple of $B$ and the $r$th multiple of $C$ the *same* multiples of $B$ and $C$.

**Art. 4.** It is necessary to prove certain propositions regarding magnitudes and multiples of magnitudes before entering upon the discussion of the relations between magnitudes.

* A point will also be denoted by a capital letter, but this will not lead to any difficulty.

### Art. 5. PROPOSITION I.* (Euc. v. 1.)

ENUNCIATION. *To prove that* $r(A+B)=rA+rB$.

Construct the following diagram.

Draw a rectangle.

Draw one line parallel to one pair of sides, dividing it into two compartments.

Draw $(r-1)$ lines parallel to the other pair of sides, dividing each of the two compartments into $r$ compartments.

In or upon each one of the upper row of compartments place the magnitude $A$; and in or upon each one of the lower compartments place the magnitude $B$.

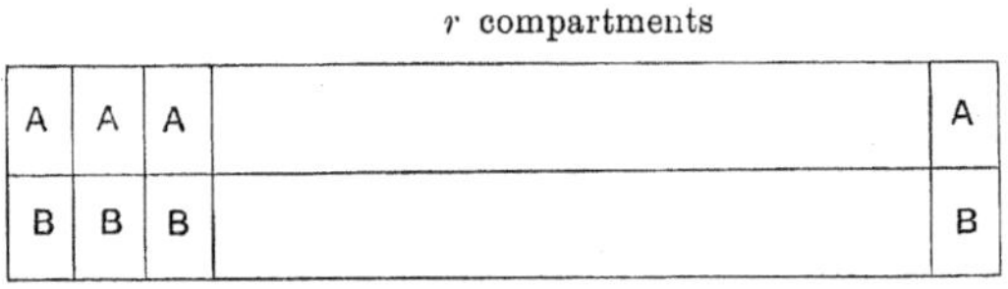

$r$ compartments

| A | A | A | | A |
|---|---|---|---|---|
| B | B | B | | B |

Fig. 1.

Then, adding together the two magnitudes in any column the result is $A+B$, and as there are $r$ columns, the sum of all the magnitudes on the whole rectangle is $r(A+B)$.

Again, adding together the magnitudes in the upper row the result is $rA$, and the sum of the magnitudes in the lower row is $rB$.

Hence the sum of all the magnitudes is $rA+rB$.

But the sum of all the magnitudes is independent of the order in which they are added.

$$\therefore\ r(A+B)=rA+rB.$$

### Art. 6. EXAMPLE 1.

By repeated application of Proposition I. prove that

$$r(A+B+\ldots+K)=rA+rB+\ldots+rK.$$

### Art. 7. PROPOSITION II.* (Euc. v. 2.)

ENUNCIATION. *To prove that* $(a+b)R=aR+bR$.

Take any rectangle.

Draw $(a+b-1)$ straight lines parallel to one pair of sides, thus dividing it into $(a+b)$ compartments.

* See Note 1.

In each of these compartments place the magnitude $R$.

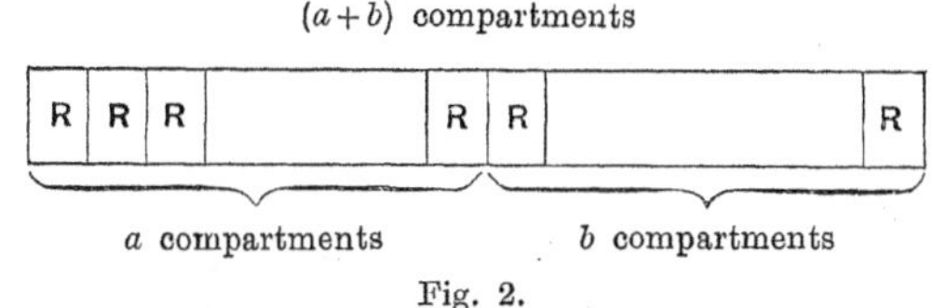


Fig. 2.

Then the sum of all the magnitudes is $(a+b)R$.

Again, separating the magnitudes into two groups, consisting respectively of the magnitudes in the first $a$ compartments, and the magnitudes in the remaining $b$ compartments, the sum of the magnitudes in the first group is $aR$, and the sum of those in the second group is $bR$.

Hence the sum of all the magnitudes is $aR + bR$.

But this sum was shown above to be $(a+b)R$.

$$\therefore\ (a+b)R = aR + bR.$$

### Art. 8. EXAMPLES.

2. Prove that $(r+s+t+\ldots+z)A = rA + sA + tA + \ldots + zA$.

3. If $A$ and $B$ are both multiples of $G$, prove that $A+B$ is a multiple of $G$.

### Art. 9. PROPOSITION III.* (Euc. v. 5.)

Enunciation. *If $A > B$, then $r(A-B) = rA - rB$.*

Since $$A > B,$$

let $$A = B + C.$$

$$\therefore\ rA = r(B+C)$$

$$= rB + rC \qquad \text{[Prop. 1.}$$

$$\therefore\ rC = rA - rB.$$

But $$C = A - B,$$

$$\therefore\ r(A-B) = rA - rB.$$

* See Note 1.

### Art. 10. PROPOSITION IV.* (Euc. v. 6.)

ENUNCIATION. *If $a > b$, prove that $(a - b) R = aR - bR$.*

Since $a > b$, and each is a positive integer,

$\therefore$ $(a - b)$ is a positive integer which may be called $c$.

$$\therefore \; a = b + c.$$

$$\therefore \; aR = (b + c) R$$

$$= bR + cR. \qquad \text{[Prop. 2.}$$

$$\therefore \; cR = aR - bR$$

$$\therefore \; (a - b) R = aR - bR.$$

### Art. 11. EXAMPLE 4.

If $A$ and $B$ are multiples of $G$, then the difference of $A$ and $B$ is a multiple of $G$.

### Art. 12. PROPOSITION V.†

ENUNCIATION. *To prove that*

$$r (sA) = rs (A) = sr (A) = s (rA).$$

Let a rectangle be drawn and divided into compartments standing in $r$ columns and $s$ rows.

Place the magnitude $A$ in each compartment.

Then the sum of the magnitudes in any row is $rA$, and the sum of those in any column is $sA$.

Since there are $s$ rows, the sum of all the magnitudes is $s (rA)$.

Since there are $r$ columns, the sum of all the magnitudes is $r (sA)$.

If the number of the magnitudes be counted, it is $rs$, or it may also be expressed as $sr$.

Hence the sum can be written in either of the forms $rs (A)$ or $sr (A)$.

But the sum of the magnitudes is the same in whatever way it is determined.

$$\therefore \; r (sA) = rs (A) = sr (A) = s (rA).$$

### Art. 13. EXAMPLE 5.

If $A$ and $B$ are multiples of $G$, then the sum and difference of $rA$ and $sB$ are multiples of $G$.

* See Note 1. † See Notes 1, 2.

## Art. 14. PROPOSITION VI (i).

ENUNCIATION. *If* $A > B$, *then* $rA > rB$;
*If* $A = B$, *then* $rA = rB$;
*If* $A < B$, *then* $rA < rB$.

If $A > B$,
let $A = B + C$.

$\therefore \; rA = r(B + C)$

$= rB + rC$ [Prop. 1.

$\therefore \; rA > rB$.

If $A = B$,
then $rA = rB$.

If $A < B$,
then $B > A$.

Hence $rB > rA$, by what is proved above.

$\therefore \; rA < rB$.

## PROPOSITION VI (ii).

ENUNCIATION. *If* $rA > rB$, *then* $A > B$;
*If* $rA = rB$, *then* $A = B$;
*If* $rA < rB$, *then* $A < B$.

If $rA > rB$,
suppose if possible that $A$ is not greater than $B$.

Then either $A = B$,
or $A < B$.

But by the first part of this proposition,
if $A = B$, then $rA = rB$;
and if $A < B$, then $rA < rB$.

Both these results are contradictory to the hypothesis that $rA > rB$.

Hence $A$ must be greater than $B$.

The second and third cases can be proved in like manner.

## Art. 15. PROPOSITION VI (iii).

ENUNCIATION. *If* $a > b$, *then* $aR > bR$;
*If* $a = b$, *then* $aR = bR$;
*If* $a < b$, *then* $aR < bR$.

If $a > b$,

let $a = b + c$,

$\therefore\ aR = (b + c) R$

$= bR + cR$; [Prop. 2.

$\therefore\ aR > bR$.

If $a = b$,

then $aR = bR$.

If $a < b$,

then $b > a$,

$\therefore\ bR > aR$, by what was proved above.

$\therefore\ aR < bR$.

## PROPOSITION VI (iv).

ENUNCIATION. *If* $aR > bR$, *then* $a > b$;
*If* $aR = bR$, *then* $a = b$;
*If* $aR < bR$, *then* $a < b$.

If $aR > bR$,

suppose if possible that $a$ is not greater than $b$.

Then either $a = b$,

or $a < b$.

But by part (iii) of this proposition,

if $a = b$, then $aR = bR$;

and if $a < b$, then $aR < bR$.

Both these results are contradictory to the hypothesis that

$aR > bR$.

Hence $a$ must be greater than $b$.

The second and third cases can be proved in like manner.

## Art. 16. EXAMPLES.

6. (i) If $aU > bV$,
$bT > cU$,
prove that $aT > cV$.

(ii) If $nrU > tV$,
and $tT > nsU$,
prove that $rT > sV$.

7.* If $rA > sB$,
and $rC < sD$,
prove that no integers $r'$, $s'$ can exist such that
$r'A < s'B$,
and $r'C > s'D$.

## Art. 17. *Def.* 2. EQUIMULTIPLES.

**If the same multiples be taken of each of two magnitudes, they are called equimultiples of the magnitudes.**

Thus $2A$ and $2B$ are equimultiples of $A$ and $B$.
„ $3A$ „ $3B$ „ „ „ „

And in general

$rA$ and $rB$ are equimultiples of $A$ and $B$.

## Art. 18. EXAMPLE 8.

Find the smallest equimultiples of 4 and 5, which differ by more than 6.

## Art. 19. GEOMETRICAL ILLUSTRATIONS OF EQUIMULTIPLES.

### First Illustration.

*To construct equimultiples of a parallelogram and its base.*

Let $ABCD$ be a parallelogram standing on the base $AB$.

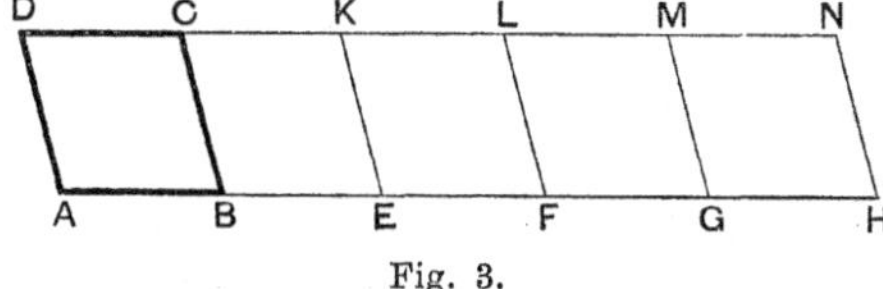


Fig. 3.

On $AB$ produced take any number of lengths $BE$, $EF$, $FG$, $GH$ each equal to $AB$, and through $E$, $F$, $G$, $H$ draw parallels to $BC$ cutting $DC$ produced in $K$, $L$, $M$, $N$ respectively.

Then the parallelograms $ABCD$, $BEKC$, $EFLK$, $FGML$, $GHNM$ are all equal because they stand on equal bases and are situated between the same parallels.

Therefore the parallelogram $AHND$ is the same multiple of the parallelogram $ABCD$ as $AH$ is of $AB$.

Therefore parallelogram $AHND$, base $AH$
are equimultiples of parallelogram $ABCD$, base $AB$.

If $AH = r(AB)$, then $AHND = r(ABCD)$.

### Art. 20. Second Illustration.

*To construct equimultiples of a triangle and its base.*

Let $ABC$ be a triangle standing on the base $AB$.

On $AB$ produced take any number of lengths $BD$, $DE$, $EF$ each equal to $AB$, and join $CD$, $CE$, $CF$.

Then the triangles $CAB$, $CBD$, $CDE$, $CEF$ all stand on equal bases, and have the same altitude.

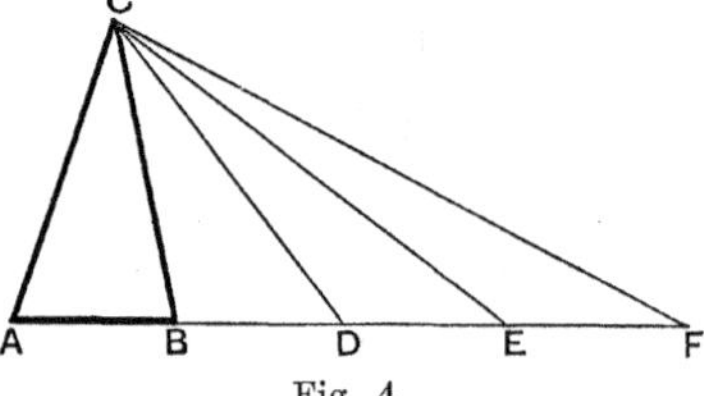

Fig. 4.

Therefore they are equal in area.

Therefore the triangle $AFC$ is the same multiple of the triangle $ABC$ as $AF$ is of $AB$.

Therefore triangle $AFC$, base $AF$
are equimultiples of triangle $ABC$, base $AB$.

If $AF = r(AB)$, then $\triangle AFC = r(\triangle ABC)$.

### Art. 21. Third Illustration.

*To construct equimultiples of the* three *magnitudes, the angle at the centre of a circle, the arc on which it stands, and the sector bounded by the arc and the sides of the angle.*

Let $O$ be the centre of a circle.

Let $AOB$ be an angle at the centre standing on the arc $AB$.

Now make any number of angles $BOC$, $COD$, $DOE$, $EOF$, $FOG$, $GOH$ each equal to $AOB$.

Then the arcs $BC$, $CD$, $DE$, $EF$, $FG$, $GH$ are each equal to the arc $AB$, because they subtend equal angles at the centre of the circle.

Hence the arc $AH$ is the same multiple of the arc $AB$ as the angle $AOH$ is of the angle $AOB$.

Therefore arc $AH$, angle $AOH$

are equimultiples of arc $AB$, angle $AOB$.

Further since each of the sectors $BOC$, $COD$, $DOE$, $EOF$, $FOG$, $GOH$ can be superposed on the sector $AOB$, they are all equal.

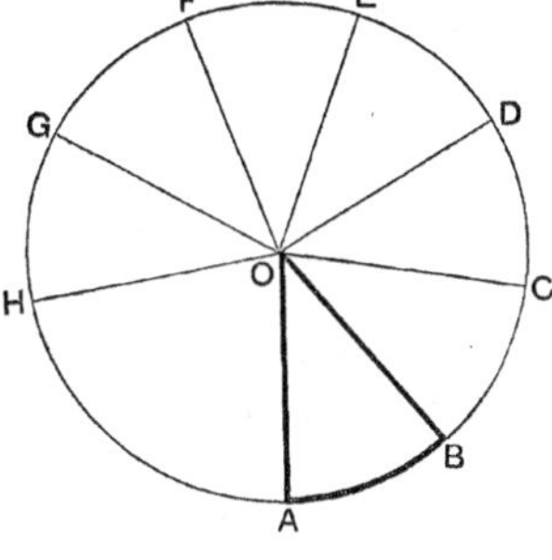

Fig. 5.

Therefore the sector $AOH$ is the same multiple of the sector $AOB$ as the angle $AOH$ is of the angle $AOB$.

Therefore sector $AOH$, angle $AOH$

are equimultiples of sector $AOB$, angle $AOB$.

Therefore

arc $AH$, angle $AOH$, sector $AOH$

are equimultiples of arc $AB$, angle $AOB$, sector $AOB$.

If arc $AH = r(\text{arc } AB)$, then $A\hat{O}H = r(A\hat{O}B)$, and sector $AOH = r(\text{sector } AOB)$.

## Art. 22. Fourth Illustration.

*To construct equimultiples of the intercepts made by two parallel straight lines on two other straight lines.*

Let the straight lines $OX$, $OY$ be cut by the parallel lines $AB$, $CD$.

To construct equimultiples of the intercepts $AC$, $BD$.

Draw any straight line $PQ$ parallel to $AB$, cutting $OX$ at $P$ and $OY$ at $Q$.

From $P$ along $PX$ set off any number of lengths $PR$, $RS$, $ST$ each equal to $AC$, and draw $TW$ parallel to $AB$ to cut $OY$ at $W$, then $PT$ and $QW$ are equimultiples of $AC$ and $BD$.

For draw $RZ$ parallel to $PQ$ to cut $OY$ at $Z$.

Draw $BE$, $QN$ parallel to $OX$ cutting $CD$ at $E$, and $RZ$ at $N$ respectively.

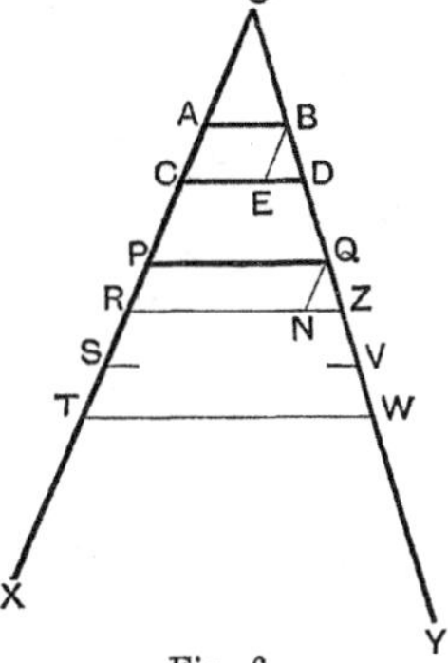

Fig. 6.

Then $BE = AC = PR = QN$

$E\hat{B}D = X\hat{O}Y = N\hat{Q}Z$

$B\hat{D}E = Q\hat{Z}N$

$\therefore$ the triangles $BED$, $NQZ$ are congruent.

$\therefore$ $BD = QZ$.

In like manner if $SV$ be drawn parallel to $AB$, $ZV$ will be equal to $BD$; and if $TW$ be drawn parallel to $AB$, $VW$ will be equal to $BD$.

Hence $PR$, $RS$, $ST$ being each equal to $AC$,

$QZ$, $ZV$, $VW$ are each equal to $BD$.

$\therefore$ $QW$ is the same multiple of $BD$ as $PT$ is of $AC$;

$\therefore$ $PT$, $QW$ are equimultiples of $AC$, $BD$.

If $PT = r(AC)$, then $QW = r(BD)$.

### Art. 23. AXIOM.

**If $A$ and $B$ are two magnitudes of the same kind, it is always possible to find a multiple of either which will exceed the other.**

This is usually known as the Axiom of Archimedes. But Euclid uses it in the Fifth Book, see Euc. v. 8, and it is also implied in the fourth definition of the Fifth Book.

### Art. 24. PROPOSITION VII. (Contained in Euc. v. 8.)

ENUNCIATION. *If $X$, $Y$, $Z$ be three magnitudes of the same kind, and if $X$ and $Y$ be unequal, then it is always possible to find equimultiples of $X$ and $Y$, such that some multiple of $Z$ lies between them.*

Since $X$ and $Y$ are unequal, one of them must be the greater.

Let $Y$ be greater than $X$.

It is to be proved that integers $n$ and $s$ exist, such that

$$nX < sZ, \text{ and } sZ < nY;$$

or more briefly,

$$nX < sZ < nY.$$

Since $Y > X$, therefore $Y - X$ is a magnitude of the same kind as $Z$.

Hence an integer $n$ exists, such that

$$n(Y - X) > Z.$$ [See Axiom, Art. 23.

$$\therefore\ nY - nX > Z.$$

$$\therefore\ nY > nX + Z.$$

Now let $tZ$ be the greatest multiple of $Z$ which does not exceed $nX$.

Then either (i) $nX = tZ$,

or (ii) $tZ < nX < (t+1)Z$.

Now (i) if $nX = tZ,$

then $nX < (t+1) Z.$

But $nY > nX + Z,$

$\therefore\ nY > tZ + Z;$

$\therefore\ nX < (t+1) Z < nY.$

(ii) If $tZ < nX < (t+1) Z,$

then $nX < (t+1) Z.$

But $nY > nX + Z,$

and $nX > tZ,$

$\therefore\ nY > (t+1) Z.$

Hence as before $nX < (t+1) Z < nY.$

Replacing $(t+1)$ by $s$, it follows that integers $n$ and $s$ exist, such that

$$nX < sZ < nY.$$

**Art. 25.** An illustration of Prop. 7 is given in Fig. 7 in the case where $X$, $Y$, $Z$ are segments of straight lines.

Here $OA$ and $OB$ are equimultiples of $X$ and $Y$, such that $AB$ is greater than $Z$, and $OC$ is a multiple of $Z$, which is greater than $OA$, but less than $OB$.

It should be noticed that $2Z$ lies between $3X$ and $3Y$, that $3Z$ lies between $4X$ and $4Y$, but this is ascertained only after the figure has been drawn, whilst the fact that a multiple of $Z$, which in this case is $4Z$, lies between $5X$ and $5Y$ is determinable from the consideration that $5(Y-X) > Z$, as in Prop. 7.

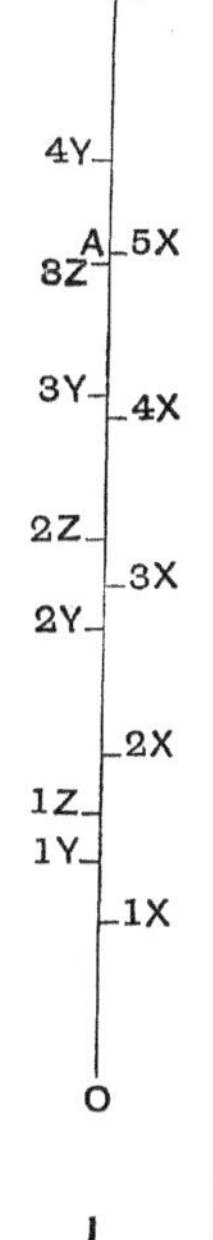


Fig. 7.

**Art. 26.** EXAMPLES.

9. Prove the converse of Prop. 7, viz. :—

If $X$, $Y$, $Z$ be three magnitudes of the same kind, and if no multiple of $Z$ can be found which is intermediate in magnitude between any equimultiples of $X$ and $Y$, then $X$ and $Y$ must be equal.

10. If $X = 4$, $Y = 5$, $Z = 6$, find from a figure the least value of $n$ for which a single multiple of $Z$ is intermediate in magnitude between $nX$ and $nY$.

Find also the least value of $n$ for which two multiples of $Z$ are intermediate in magnitude between $nX$ and $nY$.

11.* (i) If $rA > sB$,

and $rC = sD$,

prove that integers $n$, $t$ exist such that

$$nrA > tB,$$

and $$nrC < tD.$$

(ii) If $rA = sB$,

and $rC < sD$,

prove that integers $n$, $t$ exist such that

$$nrA > tB,$$
$$nrC < tD.$$

**Art. 27.** The multiples of $A$ can be arranged in order of magnitude as follows:—

$$A,\ 2A,\ 3A,\ 4A,\ \ldots,\ rA,\ \ldots$$

and this series, every term of which is known when $A$ is known, can be carried on to any extent.

### Art. 28. SCALE OF MULTIPLES OR MULTIPLE SCALE.

*Def.* 3. **The set of magnitudes**

$$A,\ 2A,\ 3A,\ 4A,\ \ldots,\ rA,\ \ldots$$

**may be called collectively the scale of the multiples of $A$, or more briefly the multiple scale of $A$.**

**Art. 29.** If $A$ and $B$ be two magnitudes of the same kind, then however small $A$ may be, or however great $B$ may be, the multiples in the scale

$$A,\ 2A,\ 3A,\ 4A,\ \ldots,\ rA,\ \ldots$$

will, after a certain multiple, all exceed $B$†.

In like manner, after a certain multiple, they will all exceed $2B$; and, so on, multiples can be found which will exceed

$$3B,\ 4B,\ \ldots,\ sB,\ \ldots.$$

Hence it is possible to determine the positions of the magnitudes

$$B,\ 2B,\ 3B,\ 4B,\ \ldots,\ sB,\ \ldots$$

with regard to the scale of the multiples of $A$.

Hence it is possible to arrange in a single series in ascending order the magnitudes occurring in the multiple scales of two magnitudes $A$ and $B$ of the same kind.

† See Axiom in Art. 23.

**Art. 30.** For example, take any two lengths $A$ and $B$ and an indefinite straight line $OX$.

Starting from a fixed point $O$ on this line, mark off lengths equal to $A$ on the left of it, and equal to $B$ on the right of it as in Figure 8. This figure can be continued upwards to any extent.

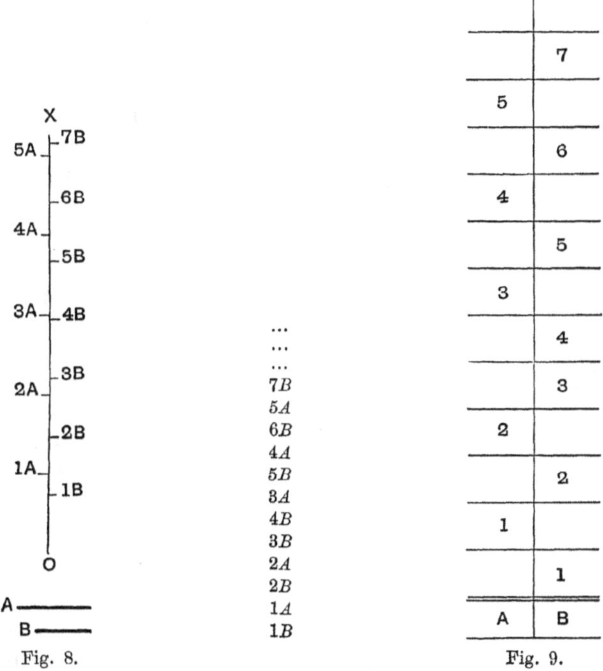


Fig. 8.

Fig. 9.

With the above values of $A$ and $B$ the magnitudes printed between Figs. 8 and 9 are in ascending order of magnitude, and they may be continued vertically upwards to any extent.

If two of the magnitudes in the series are equal, they should be placed on the same horizontal line.

Now let horizontal lines be drawn between consecutive multiples, and let the multiples of $A$ be moved to the left, there being no vertical motion.

Then let the letters $A$ and $B$ be removed.

Then let $A$ be placed below the column of figures on the left, and $B$ below the column of figures on the right.

The result is Figure 9, which can be continued vertically upwards to any extent.

**Art. 31.** *Def.* 4. RELATIVE MULTIPLE SCALE OF TWO MAGNITUDES.

**The portion of the diagram in Fig. 9 above the letters $A$ and $B$ is called the relative multiple scale of $A$, $B$; or more briefly the scale of $A$, $B$.**

It is merely a device for showing the order of the succession of the multiples of $A$ and of $B$ in a single ascending series.

The magnitude $A$ is called the first term of the scale, and $B$ the second term of the scale.

The figures above $A$ are said to stand in the first column of the scale; those above $B$ in the second column of the scale.

**Art. 32.** If a number $r$ standing in the first column is at a higher level than a number $s$ in the second column, it means that

$rA$ is greater than $sB$.

It will be convenient to indicate this last statement by drawing a diagram as in Fig. 10.

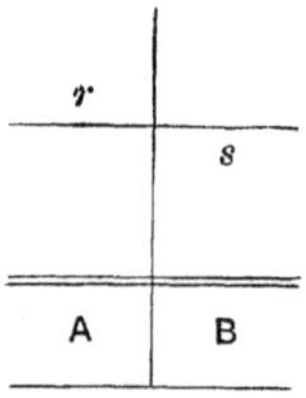

| $r$ | |
|---|---|
| | $s$ |
| A | B |

Fig. 10.

In like manner the statement that

$rA$ is equal to $sB$

may be indicated by the diagram in Fig. 11,

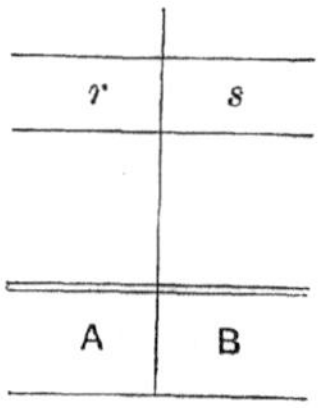

| $r$ | $s$ |
|---|---|
| A | B |

Fig. 11.

and the statement that

$rA$ is less than $sB$

may be indicated by the diagram in Fig. 12.

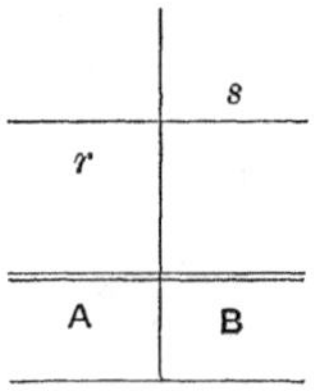

| | $s$ |
|---|---|
| $r$ | |
| A | B |

Fig. 12.

In Figures 10 and 12 the single horizontal line between $r$ and $s$ represents one or more horizontal lines in the scale of $A$, $B$.

**Art. 33.** It will be found convenient to use the following abbreviations:—

(1) "The scale of $A$, $B$" is abbreviated into $[A, B]$.

(2) "is the same as" is abbreviated into $\simeq$.

Thus the sentence

"the scale of $A$, $B$ is the same as the scale of $C$, $D$"

is abbreviated into

$$[A, B] \simeq [C, D].$$

**Art. 34.** As another example of a scale let $A$ be a segment of a straight line 3 inches long, and $B$ a segment of a straight line 4 inches long, then the magnitudes printed on the left of Fig. 13 are in ascending order of magnitude. Equal magnitudes are placed on the same horizontal line.

The relative multiple scale of $A$, $B$ will be found in Figure 13.

As another example the relative multiple scale of lines 5 and 6 inches long respectively is given in Figure 14.

. .
. .
. .
$9A$
$8A$, $6B$
$7A$
$5B$
$6A$
$4B$
$5A$
$4A$, $3B$
$3A$
$2B$
$2A$
$1B$
$1A$

| | |
|---|---|
| 9 | |
| 8 | 6 |
| 7 | |
| | 5 |
| 6 | |
| | 4 |
| 5 | |
| 4 | 3 |
| 3 | |
| | 2 |
| 2 | |
| | 1 |
| 1 | |
| 3 | 4 |

Fig. 13.

| | |
|---|---|
| | 6 |
| 7 | |
| 6 | 5 |
| 5 | |
| | 4 |
| 4 | |
| | 3 |
| 3 | |
| | 2 |
| 2 | |
| | 1 |
| 1 | |
| 5 | 6 |

Fig. 14.

**Art. 35.** If the scale of $A$, $B$ is the same as that of $C$, $D$, take any integer $r$ in the first column, and any integer $s$ in the second column.

Then there are three alternatives. In both scales

(i) $r$ is above $s$,

or (ii) $r$ is on the same level as $s$,

or (iii) $r$ is below $s$.

If $r$ is above $s$, then this indicates that

$$rA > sB,$$

and at the same time $$rC > sD;$$

and the corresponding figures are

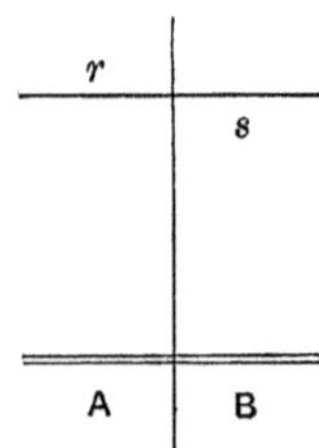


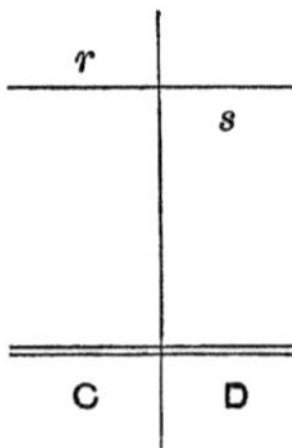


Fig. 15.

If $r$ is on the same level as $s$, then this indicates that

$$rA = sB,$$

and at the same time $$rC = sD;$$

and the corresponding figures are

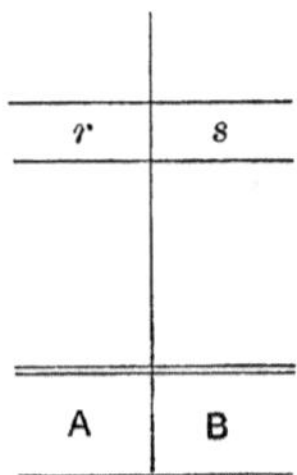


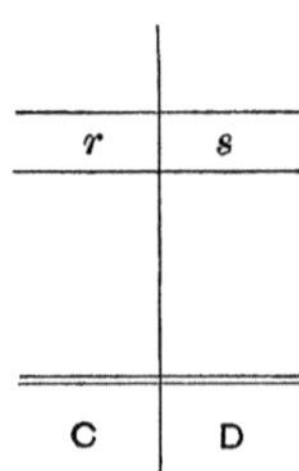


Fig. 16.

If $r$ is below $s$, then this indicates that

$$rA < sB,$$

and at the same time $$rC < sD;$$

and the corresponding figures are

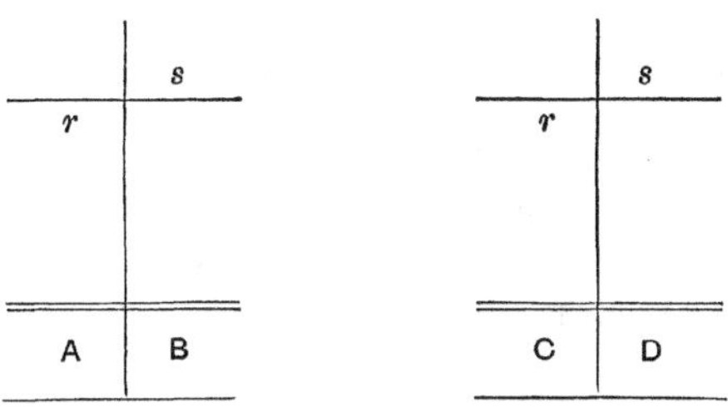


Fig. 17.

Hence if the scale of $A, B$ is the same as that of $C, D$ and if for any value of the integers $r$ and $s$ it is found that

$$rA > sB,$$

then $r$ is above $s$ in the scale of $A, B$.

Hence $r$ is above $s$ in the scale of $C, D$.

$$\therefore \; rC > sD.$$

Hence if $rA > sB$, then $rC > sD$. (1)

In like manner if $rC > sD$, then $rA > sB$, (2)

if $rA = sB$, then $rC = sD$, (3)

if $rC = sD$, then $rA = sB$, (4)

if $rA < sB$, then $rC < sD$, (5)

if $rC < sD$, then $rA < sB$. (6)

It is to be noted that these six conditions must be satisfied for every value of the integer $r$ and every value of the integer $s$ (not merely for some single value of the integer $r$ and some single value of the integer $s$).

The whole six conditions are not however all independent of one another. They will all hold if (1), (3) and (5) hold; or if (2), (4) and (6) hold; or if (1), (2), (5) and (6) hold as will now be shown.

## Art. 36. PROPOSITION VIII. (i).

FIRST FORM OF THE CONDITIONS THAT TWO SCALES MAY BE THE SAME.

*If all values of r, s which make*

(1) $rA > sB$, *also make* $rC > sD$;

(2) $rA = sB$, *also make* $rC = sD$;

(3) $rA < sB$, *also make* $rC < sD$;

*then conversely will all values of r, s which make*

(4) $rC > sD$, *also make* $rA > sB$;

(5) $rC = sD$, *also make* $rA = sB$;

(6) $rC < sD$, *also make* $rA < sB$;

*and therefore the scale of A, B will be the same as that of C, D.*

Suppose if possible values of $r$, $s$ exist which make $rC > sD$ but do not make $rA > sB$.

Then either $rA = sB$,

or $rA < sB$.

If $rA = sB$, then by (2) $rC = sD$, which is contrary to the hypothesis that $rC > sD$.

If $rA < sB$, then by (3) $rC < sD$, which is also contrary to the hypothesis.

Hence if $rC > sD$, then must $rA > sB$.

Hence the condition (4) is involved in the conditions (1), (2) and (3).

In like manner it follows that the conditions (5) and (6) are also involved in the conditions (1), (2) and (3).

Hence the scale of $A$, $B$ is the same as that of $C$, $D$.

## Art. 37. PROPOSITION VIII. (ii).

SECOND FORM OF THE CONDITIONS THAT TWO SCALES MAY BE THE SAME*.

*If all values of the integers r, s which make*

(1) $rA > sB$, *also make* $rC > sD$;

(2) $rA < sB$, *also make* $rC < sD$;

(3) $rC > sD$, *also make* $rA > sB$;

(4) $rC < sD$, *also make* $rA < sB$;

* See Stolz, *Vorlesungen über Allgemeine Arithmetik*, Part I., p. 87.

*then if there are any values of the integers r, s which make*

(5) $rA = sB$, *they must also make* $rC = sD$;

(6) $rC = sD$, *they must also make* $rA = sB$;

*and therefore the scale of A, B is the same as that of C, D.*

Suppose if possible that some values of $r$, $s$ exist which make $rA = sB$, but $rC$ not equal to $sD$.

Then either $$rC > sD,$$
or $$rC < sD.$$

If $$rC > sD,$$
then by (3) it follows that $$rA > sB,$$
which is contrary to the hypothesis that
$$rA = sB.$$

If $$rC < sD,$$
then by (4) it follows that $$rA < sB,$$
which is contrary to the hypothesis that
$$rA = sB.$$

Consequently $rC$ is neither greater nor less than $sD$.

Hence if $rA = sB$, then $rC = sD$.

In like manner if $rC = sD$, then $rA = sB$.

Consequently the scale of $A$, $B$ is the same as that of $C$, $D$.

## Art. 38. EXAMPLES.

12. If for a *single* value of the integer $r$, say $r_1$, and a *single* value of the integer $s$, say $s_1$, it is true that
$$r_1 A = s_1 B$$
and $$r_1 C = s_1 D,$$
then prove that *any* values of the integers $r$, $s$ which make

(1) $rA > sB$, also make $rC > sD$,

(2) $rA = sB$, also make $rC = sD$,

(3) $rA < sB$, also make $rC < sD$.

13.* If $$rA < sB,$$
if $$rC > sE,$$
if $$tA > uB,$$
if $$tC < uF;$$
and if further $$[A, B] \simeq [C, D],$$
prove that $$E < D < F.$$

## Art. 39. *Def.* 5. THE IDENTICAL SCALE.

If
$$A = B,$$
then
$$rA = rB.$$

Hence in the scale of $A$, $B$, the number $r$ in the first column is always on the same level as the same number $r$ in the second column. Hence the scale of $A$, $A$ is

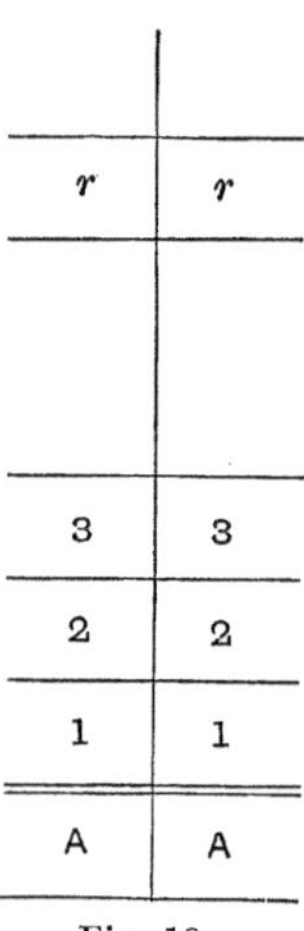


Fig. 18.

This is called the Identical Scale.

## Art. 40. EXAMPLES.

14. Form the relative multiple scale of
   (1) lines 7 inches long and 8 inches long respectively,
   (2) lines 8 inches long and 9 inches long respectively.

How far are the two scales the same?

15. Let $A$ be the side of a square, and $B$ its diagonal; form the relative multiple scale of $A$ and $B$ far enough to show that the tenth multiple of $B$ lies between the fourteenth and fifteenth multiples of $A$.

16. Let $A$ be the side of a square, and $B$ be the hypotenuse of a right-angled triangle, one of whose sides is $A$ and the other is the diagonal of the square. Form the relative multiple scale of $A$ and $B$ far enough to show that the tenth multiple of $B$ lies between the seventeenth and eighteenth multiples of $A$.

17. Let $A$ be the diagonal of a square, and $B$ be the hypotenuse of a right-angled triangle, one of whose sides is $A$ and the other is a side of the square. Form the relative multiple scale of $A$ and $B$ far enough to show that the tenth multiple of $B$ lies between the twelfth and thirteenth multiples of $A$.

# SECTION II.

THE SIMPLER PROPOSITIONS IN THE THEORY OF RELATIVE MULTIPLE SCALES WITH GEOMETRICAL APPLICATIONS. FIRST SERIES. Nos. 9–16.

### Art. 41. PROPOSITION IX.* (Euc. V. 15.)

ENUNCIATION 1. *To prove that the scale of $A$, $B$ is the same as the scale of $nA$, $nB$,*

*i.e.* $$[A, B] \simeq [nA, nB].$$

ENUNCIATION 2. To prove that two magnitudes have to one another the same ratio as their equimultiples,

i.e. $$A : B = nA : nB.$$

Take any integers $r$, $s$ in the first and second columns respectively of the scale of $A$, $B$.

There are three alternatives, represented by the figures

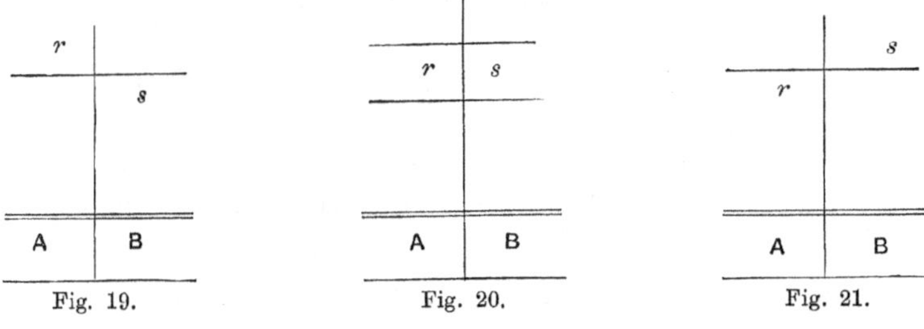


Fig. 19. Fig. 20. Fig. 21.

which severally express the facts

$$rA > sB \qquad rA = sB \qquad rA < sB$$

from which follow

$$nrA > nsB \qquad nrA = nsB \qquad nrA < nsB$$

$$\therefore\ r(nA) > s(nB) \qquad r(nA) = s(nB) \qquad r(nA) < s(nB)$$

* See Note 3.

which are represented in the scale of $nA$, $nB$ by the figures

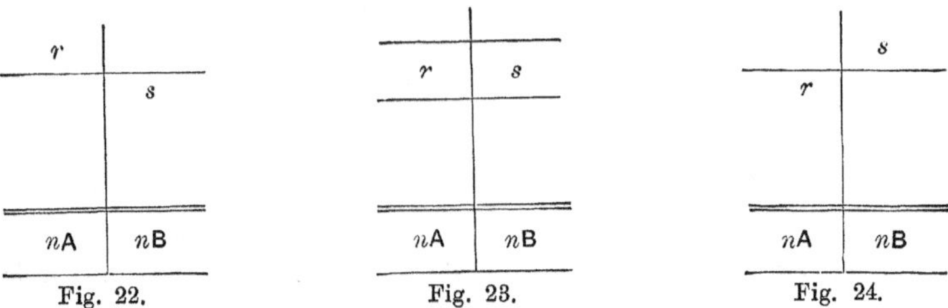

Fig. 22. Fig. 23. Fig. 24.

Comparing the Figures 22, 23, 24 with the Figures 19, 20, 21 respectively, it follows at once that

the scale of $A, B$ is the same as that of $nA$, $nB$*.

**Art. 42.** The case of the above Proposition in which $n = 2$ will often be required,

i.e. $$[A, B] \simeq [2A, 2B].$$

**Art. 43.** Since $n$ represents any whole number whatever, it may have an infinite number of values.

Hence $nA$ and $nB$ represent an infinite number of pairs of magnitudes, e.g. $2A$ and $2B$, $3A$ and $3B$,...... such that the scale of any pair is the same as that of $A$, $B$.

Hence there are an infinite number of pairs of magnitudes which have the same scale.

Hence if a scale be given, the magnitudes of which it is the scale are not given.

Thus two magnitudes of the same kind determine a definite scale; but if a scale only be given, the magnitudes of which it is the scale are not given.

### Art. 44. Arithmetical Application of Proposition IX.

Let $r$ and $s$ be two whole numbers.

Let the number $r$ be divided into $s$ equal parts, and let each part be denoted by the symbol $\frac{r}{s}$.

* If $A$ and $B$ are numbers, then denoting numbers by small letters it follows that

$$[r, s] \simeq [nr, ns].$$

Then $$s\left(\frac{r}{s}\right) = r,$$
and $$s(1) = s.$$
Now by Prop. 9, $$[A, B] \simeq [nA, nB].$$
Take $$A = \frac{r}{s},$$
$$B = 1,$$
and $$n = s.$$
Then $$\left[\frac{r}{s}, 1\right] \simeq [r, s].$$

Hence the relative multiple scale of the two numbers $r$, $s$ determines the rational fraction which is denoted by the symbol $\frac{r}{s}$.

Although the term "ratio" has not yet been defined it may here be stated that the rational fraction $\frac{r}{s}$ is taken to be the measure of the ratio of $r$ to $s$.

## Art. 45. PROPOSITION X. (Euc. V. 11.)

ENUNCIATION 1.

*If the scale of A, B is the same as that of C, D;*
*and if the scale of A, B is the same as that of E, F;*
*then the scale of C, D is the same as that of E, F;*

*i.e. if* $$[A, B] \simeq [C, D],$$
*and if* $$[A, B] \simeq [E, F],$$
*then* $$[C, D] \simeq [E, F].$$

ENUNCIATION 2. Ratios which are equal to the same ratio are equal to one another,

i.e. if $$A : B = C : D,$$
and $$A : B = E : F,$$
then $$C : D = E : F.$$

There is a certain scale, viz.:—that of $A$, $B$.

The scale of $C$, $D$ consists of the same arrangement of numbers as that of $A$, $B$.

So also does the scale of $E$, $F$.

Hence the scale of $C$, $D$ is the same arrangement of numbers as the scale of $E$, $F$.

$$\therefore\ [C, D] \simeq [E, F].$$

### Art. 46. *Def.* 6. MEASURE.

**If a magnitude *A* contains another magnitude *B* an exact number of times, *B* is said to be a measure of *A*.**

### Art. 47. *Def.* 7. COMMON MEASURE.

**If the magnitudes *A* and *B* each contain another magnitude *G* an exact number of times, then *G* is said to be a common measure of *A* and *B*.**

### Art. 48. *Def.* 8. COMMENSURABLE MAGNITUDES.

**If two magnitudes have a common measure they are said to be commensurable.**

### Art. 49. PROPOSITION XI. (Euc. X. 5.)

ENUNCIATION 1. *The scale of two commensurable magnitudes is the same as that of two whole numbers.*

ENUNCIATION 2. Commensurable magnitudes are to one another in the ratio of two whole numbers.

Let $A$ and $B$ be two commensurable magnitudes.

Let $N$ be their common measure.

Then

$$A = aN,$$
$$B = bN,$$

where $a$, $b$ are some two whole numbers.

It will now be proved that $[A, B] \simeq [a, b]$.

Take any integers $r$ in the first column, $s$ in the second column of the scale of $A$, $B$.

Then there are three alternatives represented by the figures

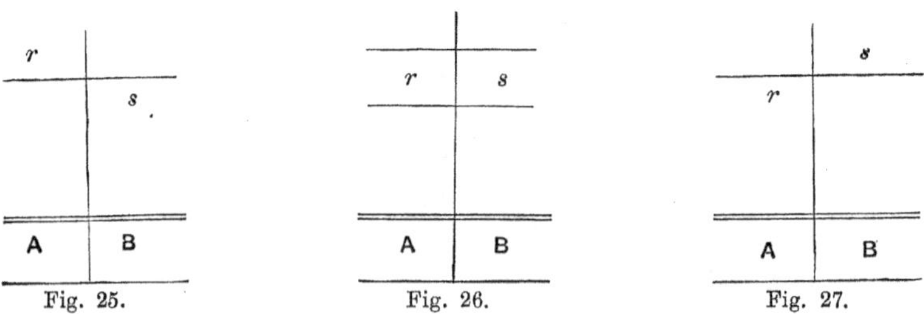


Fig. 25. Fig. 26. Fig. 27.

which severally express the facts

| | | |
|---|---|---|
| $rA > sB$ | $rA = sB$ | $rA < sB$ |
| $\therefore\ raN > sbN$ | $\therefore\ raN = sbN$ | $\therefore\ raN < sbN$ |
| $\therefore\ ra > sb$ | $\therefore\ ra = sb$ | $\therefore\ ra < sb$ [Prop. VI. (iv) |

These are represented in the scale of $a$, $b$ by the figures

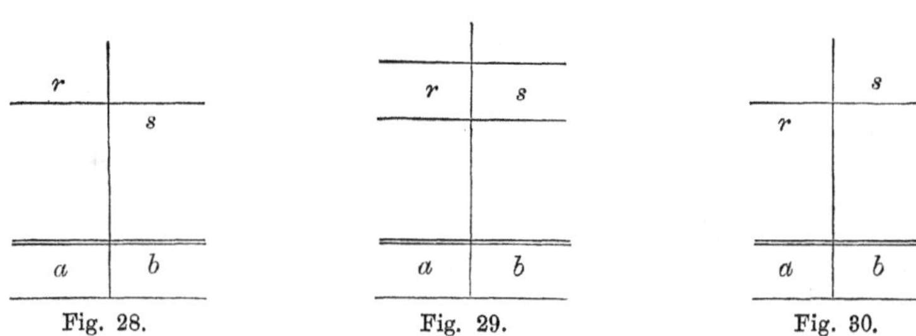


Fig. 28. Fig. 29. Fig. 30.

Comparing Figure 28 with Figure 25,
" Figure 29 with Figure 26,
and Figure 30 with Figure 27,
it follows that $$[A, B] \simeq [a, b].$$

**Art. 50.** The above proposition expresses the fact that

$$[aN, bN] \simeq [a, b].$$

Now $$[a, b] \simeq \left[\frac{a}{b}, 1\right],$$ [Art. 44.

$$\therefore [aN, bN] \simeq \left[\frac{a}{b}, 1\right].$$ [Prop. 10.

**Art. 51.** On comparing Props. 9 and 11,
viz. Prop. 9, $$[nA, nB] \simeq [A, B],$$
and Prop. 11, $$[aN, bN] \simeq [a, b],$$
it is seen that magnitudes in either are replaced by whole numbers in the other.

### Art. 52. EXAMPLE 18.

Prove the converse of Prop. 11, viz.:—

If the scale of two magnitudes is the same as that of two whole numbers, then the magnitudes are commensurable.

## Art. 53. PROPOSITION XII.

ENUNCIATION. *To show that if $A$, $B$, $C$ are three magnitudes of the same kind, and if $A$ is not equal to $B$, then the scale of $A$, $C$ is not the same as that of $B$, $C$.*

If $A$ and $B$ are unequal, one of them is the greater.

Let $A$ be greater than $B$.

Then integers $r$, $n$ exist such that

$$rA > nC > rB, \qquad \text{[Prop. 7.}$$

$$\therefore \; rA > nC,$$

but $$rB < nC.$$

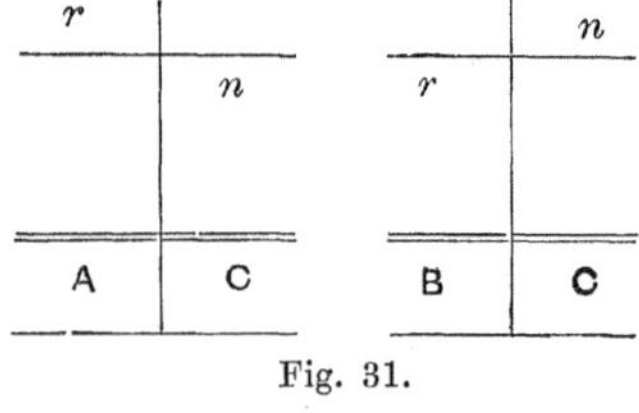

Fig. 31.

If now (see Fig. 31) the scale of $A$, $C$ be formed, $r$ standing in the first column is higher than $n$ standing in the second column.

But in the scale of $B$, $C$ (see Fig. 31), $r$ standing in the first column is lower than $n$ standing in the second column.

Hence the scale of $A$, $C$ is different from that of $B$, $C$*.

## Art. 54. *Def.* 9. CORRESPONDING POINTS AND SEGMENTS ON TWO STRAIGHT LINES.

**When two straight lines are cut by a single system of parallel straight lines, it is convenient to call the two points, in which one of the parallel straight lines cuts the two straight lines, *corresponding* points; and to call the segments of the two straight lines between any pair of the parallel straight lines *corresponding* segments.**

**Note.** If the two straight lines intersect, the point of intersection on one straight line will correspond to itself on the other straight line.

* See Note 4.

**Art. 55. PROPOSITION XIII.** **(Containing the first part of Euc. VI. 2.)**

ENUNCIATION 1. *If two straight lines be cut by any number of parallel straight lines, to prove that the scale of any two segments of one line is the same as that of the corresponding segments of the other line.*

ENUNCIATION 2. If two straight lines be cut by any number of parallel straight lines, to prove that the ratio of any two segments of one line is equal to that of the corresponding segments of the other line.

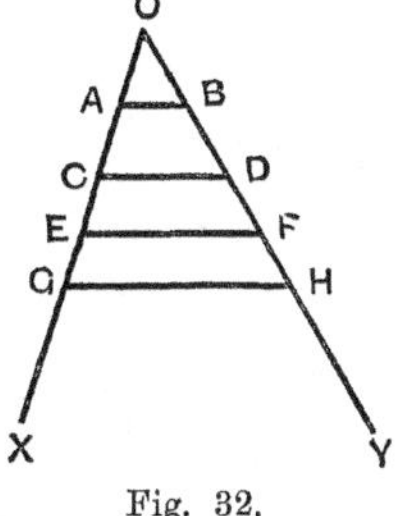

Fig. 32.

Let the intersecting lines $OX$, $OY$ be cut by the parallel straight lines $AB$, $CD$, $EF$, $GH$.

Then the segment $AC$ corresponds to the segment $BD$,

and the segment $EG$ corresponds to the segment $FH$.

It is required to prove that

$$[AC, EG] \simeq [BD, FH].$$

Take any integer $r$ in the first column, and any integer $s$ in the second column of the scale of $AC$, $EG$.

Then there are three alternatives shown by the figures

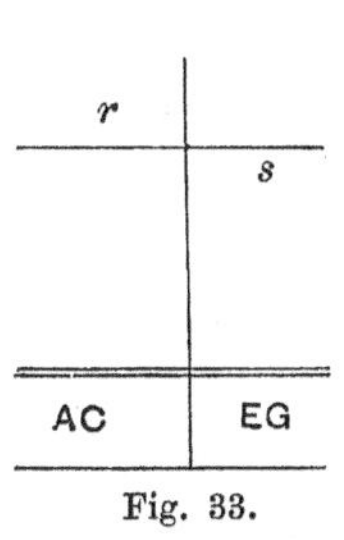

Fig. 33.

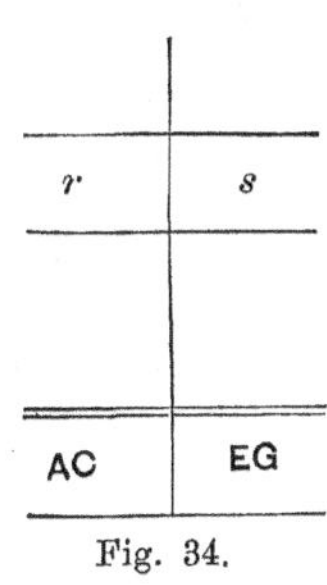

Fig. 34.

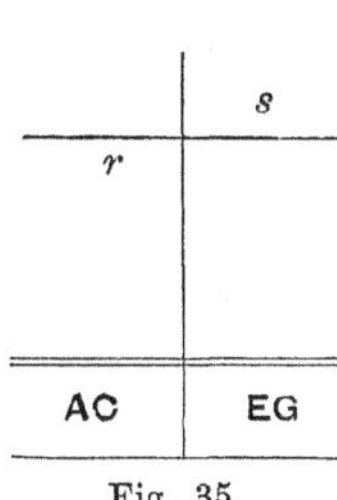

Fig. 35.

which express the facts

$$r(AC) > s(EG) \qquad r(AC) = s(EG) \qquad r(AC) < s(EG).$$

Then in order that the scale of $AC$, $EG$ may be the same as that of $BD$, $FH$ it is necessary to show that in these several cases

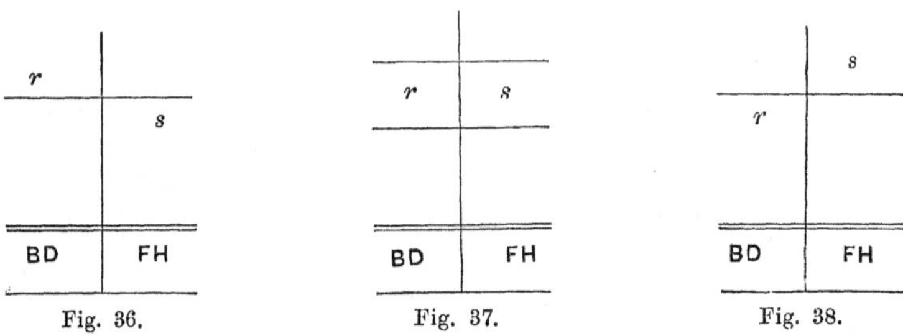


Fig. 36. Fig. 37. Fig. 38.

which express the facts

$r(BD) > s(FH)$ $\qquad r(BD) = s(FH)$ $\qquad r(BD) < s(FH)$.

On $GX$ set off a length $GK$ equal to $r(AC)$, then draw $KL$ parallel to $AB$ cutting $HY$ at $L$, then it is known by Art. 22 that $HL$ is equal to $r(BD)$.

Also on $GX$ set off a length $GM$ equal to $s(EG)$.

Then draw $MN$ parallel to $AB$ cutting $HY$ at $N$.

Then it is known by Art. 22 that $HN$ is equal to $s(FH)$.

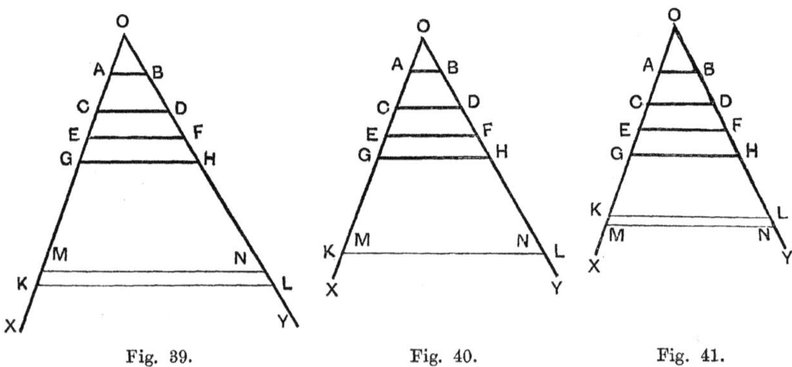


Fig. 39. Fig. 40. Fig. 41.

Since $KL$, $MN$ are both parallel to $AB$, they are parallel to one another.

Therefore $M$ and $N$ are on the same side of $KL$.

Hence in the several figures

| | | | | | |
|---|---|---|---|---|---|
| If | $GK > GM$ | If | $GK = GM$ the straight lines $KL$, $MN$ coincide. | If | $GK < GM$ |
| then | $HL > HN$ | | $\therefore\ HL = HN$ | then | $HL < HN$ |
| i.e. if | $r(AC) > s(EG)$ | i.e. if | $r(AC) = s(EG)$ | i.e. if | $r(AC) < s(EG)$ |
| then | $r(BD) > s(FH)$ | then | $r(BD) = s(FH)$ | then | $r(BD) < s(FH)$ |
| i.e. the fact expressed by Fig. 36 is a consequence of that expressed by Fig. 33. | | i.e. the fact expressed by Fig. 37 is a consequence of that expressed by Fig. 34. | | i.e. the fact expressed by Fig. 38 is a consequence of that expressed by Fig. 35. | |

Hence the scale of $AC$, $EG$ is the same as the scale of $BD$, $FH$.

### Art. 56. COROLLARY.

As a particular case of the preceding, it follows that *if $ABC$ be a triangle, and if the sides $AB$, $AC$ be cut by any straight line parallel to $BC$, then the sides $AB$, $AC$ are divided proportionally.*

Let $DE$, parallel to $BC$, cut $AB$ at $D$ and $AC$ at $E$.

There are three varieties of figure.

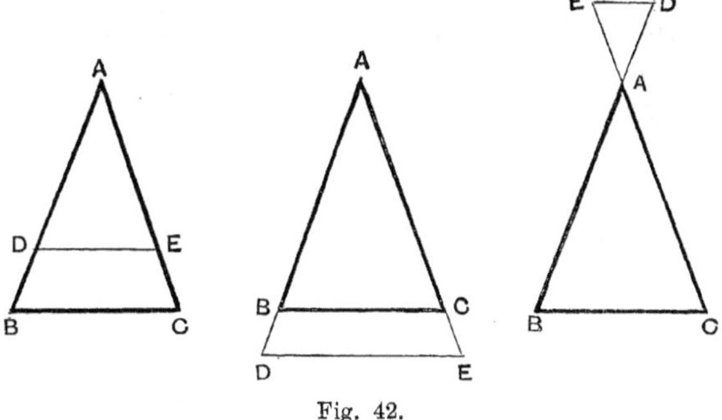


Fig. 42.

| | | | | | |
|---|---|---|---|---|---|
| The point | $A$ | corresponds | to the | point | $A$ |
| " " | $B$ | " | " | " | $C$ |
| " " | $D$ | " | " | " | $E$ |
| The segment | $AB$ | " | " | segment | $AC$ |
| " " | $AD$ | " | " | " | $AE$ |
| " " | $BD$ | " | " | " | $CE$. |

### Art. 58. COROLLARY TO PROP. XIV. (Euc. VI. 11.)

ENUNCIATION 1. *Given two straight lines, to find a third such that the scale of the first and second is the same as that of the second and third.*

ENUNCIATION 2. To find a third proportional* to two given straight lines.

This is the particular case of the above Proposition in which $EF = CD$.

### Art. 59. *Def.* 10. SIMILARLY DIVIDED STRAIGHT LINES.

**Two straight lines are said to be similarly divided, when the scale of any two parts of one straight line is the same as that of the two corresponding parts of the other straight line.**

### Art. 60. PROPOSITION XV. (Euc. VI. 10.)

ENUNCIATION. *To divide a straight line similarly to a given divided straight line.*

It is required to divide the given straight line $AB$ in the same way as the line $CF$ is divided at $D$ and $E$.

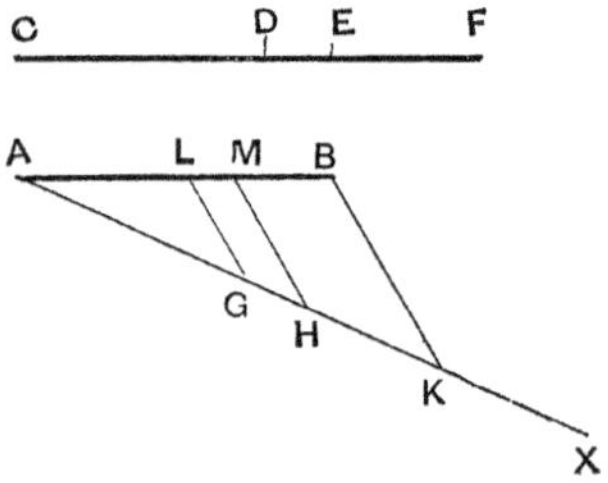

Through $A$ draw any straight line $AX$ (not in the same straight line as $AB$), and on it measure off $AG = CD$, $GH = DE$, $HK = EF$.

Join $BK$, and draw $GL$, $HM$ parallel to $BK$ cutting $AB$ in $L$, $M$ respectively.

Then since $GL$, $HM$, $BK$ are parallel lines, the segments $AG$, $AL$ correspond; so do $GH$, $LM$; and $HK$, $MB$.

C D E F
A L M B
G H K X

Fig. 44.

$\therefore\ [AL, LM] \simeq [AG, GH]$ [Prop. 13.

$\simeq [CD, DE]$.

Also $[LM, MB] \simeq [GH, HK]$ [Prop. 13.

$\simeq [DE, EF]$,

and so on.

Hence $AB$ is divided similarly to $CF$.

* See Art. 66.

### Art. 58. COROLLARY TO PROP. XIV. (Euc. VI. 11.)

ENUNCIATION 1. *Given two straight lines, to find a third such that the scale of the first and second is the same as that of the second and third.*

ENUNCIATION 2. To find a third proportional* to two given straight lines.

This is the particular case of the above Proposition in which $EF = CD$.

### Art. 59. *Def.* 10. SIMILARLY DIVIDED STRAIGHT LINES.

**Two straight lines are said to be similarly divided, when the scale of any two parts of one straight line is the same as that of the two corresponding parts of the other straight line.**

### Art. 60. PROPOSITION XV. (Euc. VI. 10.)

ENUNCIATION. *To divide a straight line similarly to a given divided straight line.*

It is required to divide the given straight line $AB$ in the same way as the line $CF$ is divided at $D$ and $E$.

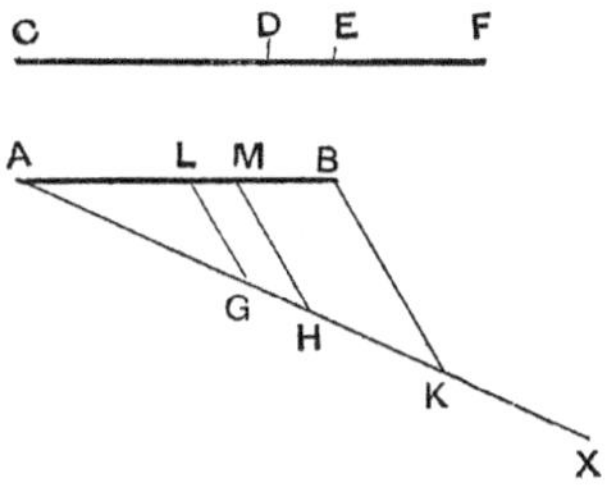

Through $A$ draw any straight line $AX$ (not in the same straight line as $AB$), and on it measure off $AG = CD$, $GH = DE$, $HK = EF$.

Join $BK$, and draw $GL$, $HM$ parallel to $BK$ cutting $AB$ in $L$, $M$ respectively.

C D E F
A L M B
G H K X

Fig. 44.

Then since $GL$, $HM$, $BK$ are parallel lines, the segments $AG$, $AL$ correspond; so do $GH$, $LM$; and $HK$, $MB$.

$\therefore\ [AL, LM] \simeq [AG, GH]$ [Prop. 13.

$\simeq [CD, DE]$.

Also $[LM, MB] \simeq [GH, HK]$ [Prop. 13.

$\simeq [DE, EF]$,

and so on.

Hence $AB$ is divided similarly to $CF$.

* See Art. 66.

### Art. 61. PROPOSITION XVI. (Euc. VI. 9.)

ENUNCIATION. *From a given straight line to cut off any part required.*

Let $AB$ be a given straight line.

From $A$ draw any straight line $AX$ (not in the same straight line as $AB$).

In $AX$ take any point $C$, and set off consecutive lengths on $AX$ each equal to $AC$, until some point $H$ is reached, such that $AH$ is the same multiple of $AC$ as $AB$ is of the part required to be cut off from it.

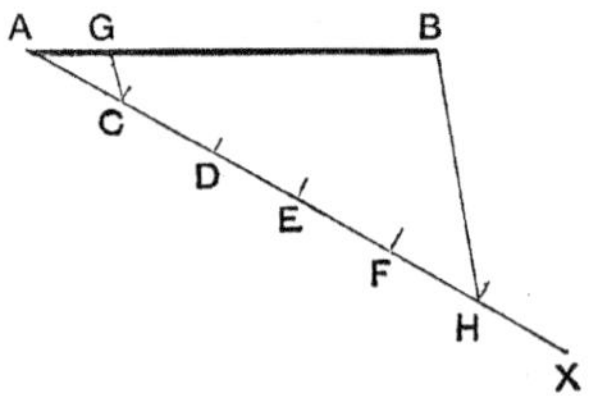

Join $BH$.

Draw $CG$ parallel to $BH$ cutting $AB$ at $G$.

Then $[AH, AC] \simeq [AB, AG]$. [Prop. 13.

Fig. 45.

Suppose that $AH = n(AC)$.

Then the scale of $AH$, $AC$ will contain the fact shown by the following figure.

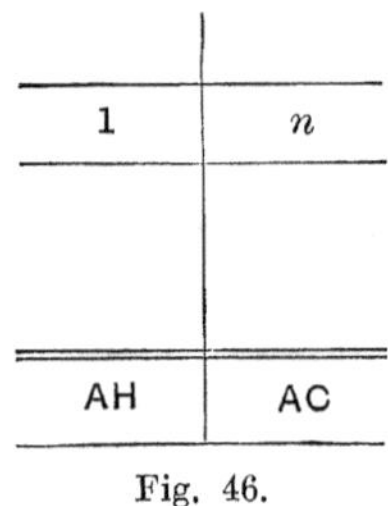


Fig. 46.

But this is also the scale of $AB$, $AG$.

Hence in the scale of $AB$, $AG$ there is the figure

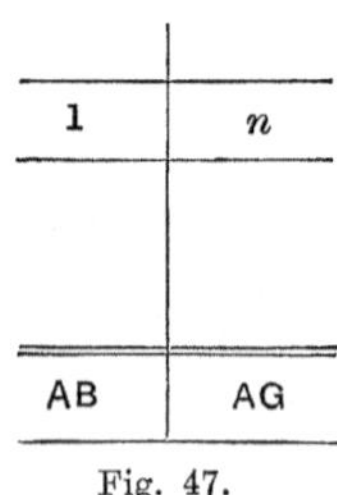


Fig. 47.

which expresses the fact $AB = n(AG)$.

Hence $AG$ is the required part of $AB$.

# SECTION III.

## A CHAPTER ON RATIO.

**Art. 62.** It is necessary now to attempt to give an answer to the question, "What is ratio?" in order that the reader may have some idea of the sense in which the term "ratio" is employed, but he is cautioned against regarding the definition about to be given as a matter of fundamental importance. It is only an endeavour to express in English the idea contained in the definition of ratio as stated in Euclid's Greek. It is not to be supposed that it will give the idea of ratio to anyone who does not already possess it, and no use will be made of the definition in the argument.

Without attempting to define what magnitudes of the same kind are, (an attempt which would only confuse the beginner,) it will be asserted first that only magnitudes which are of the same kind can have a ratio to one another.

It will be assumed next that the reader has an idea of relative magnitude.

This is probably all the assistance that can be given in understanding the following definition of ratio.

### *Def.* 11. RATIO.

**"The ratio of one magnitude to another (which must be of the same kind as the first) is the relative magnitude of the first compared with the second."**

**Art. 63.** The reader can however see that the results of Props. 9, 11, and 12 correspond with the ideas, so far as they have assumed a definite form, which he must have already formed of ratio.

To Prop. 9 corresponds the idea that the ratio of $A$ to $B$ is the same as that of $2A$ to $2B$, of $3A$ to $3B$, and so on.

To Prop. 11 corresponds the idea that the ratio of $aN$ to $bN$ is the same as that of $a$ to $b$, including as particular cases, the ratio of $2N$ to $3N$ is the same as that of 2 to 3, the ratio of $5G$ to $9G$ is the same as that of 5 to 9, and so on.

To Prop. 12 corresponds the idea that if $A$ and $B$ are different, then the ratio of $A$ to $C$ is different from that of $B$ to $C$.

These results taken together suggest, *but do not prove,* the truth of the proposition that a relative multiple scale determines a ratio and therefore also the measure of the ratio.

**Art. 64.** The proposition just mentioned depends on the Fundamental Proposition in the Theory of Relative Multiple Scales, which is as follows:—

*If $A$ and $B$ be any two magnitudes of the same kind, and if $D$ be any other magnitude; then there exists one and only one magnitude $C$ of the same kind as $D$, such that the scale of $C$, $D$ is the same as the scale of $A$, $B$**.

Assuming the truth of this proposition, let $D$ be taken as the unit of number and represented by unity, then there exists a magnitude $\rho$ of the same kind as the unit of number, such that the scale of $\rho$, 1 is the same as the scale of $A$, $B$†.

Since the magnitude $\rho$ is of the same kind as the unit of number, it may properly be called a real number.

Since $\rho$ is wholly determined by the scale of $A$, $B$ it follows that any pair of magnitudes, which have the same scale as $A$, $B$, would also determine the same number $\rho$.

Let therefore $\rho$ be taken as the measure of the ratio of any pair of magnitudes having the same scale as $A$, $B$.

This implies that $\rho$ is taken as the measure of the ratio of $\rho$ to 1, because the scale of $A$, $B$ is the same as the scale of $\rho$, 1.

## **Art. 65.** NOTATION FOR RATIO.

If two magnitudes of the same kind be called $A$ and $B$, then the ratio of $A$ to $B$ is written $A : B$.

$A$ is called the antecedent or first term of the ratio, whilst $B$ is called the consequent or second term of the ratio.

In this book, the fact that one ratio $A : B$ is equal to another ratio $C : D$ will be expressed thus:—

$$A : B = C : D,$$

and not as it is written in most modern editions of Euclid:—

$$A : B :: C : D,$$

which is read: the ratio of $A$ to $B$ is the same as the ratio of $C$ to $D$, or more briefly, $A$ is to $B$ as $C$ to $D$.

* Prop. 14 is a particular case of this.

† In the case where $A$ and $B$ have a common measure the value of $\rho$ has been actually determined, see Art. 50.

### Art. 66. *Def.* 12. PROPORTION.

**If there are four magnitudes such that the ratio of the first magnitude to the second is the same as that of the third magnitude to the fourth, then the four magnitudes are said to be proportionals, or in proportion.**

If $A$, $B$, $C$, $D$ are four magnitudes, such that

$$A : B = C : D,$$

then $A$, $B$, $C$, $D$ are proportionals.

$A$ and $D$ are called the extremes of the proportion.

$B$ and $C$ are called the means of the proportion.

$D$ is called the fourth proportional to $A$, $B$ and $C$.

The antecedents $A$ and $C$ of the two equal ratios are said to be *corresponding** terms of the ratios; so also are the consequents $B$ and $D$.

The case in which the means of the proportion are equal to one another requires special notice.

If $$X : Y = Y : Z,$$

then the three magnitudes $X$, $Y$, $Z$ are said to be in proportion; $Y$ is said to be a mean proportional between $X$ and $Z$, and $Z$ is said to be a third proportional to $X$ and $Y$.

### Art. 67. *Def.* 13. EUCLID'S TEST FOR EQUAL RATIOS.

Euclid states this Test in the following manner:—

**The first of four magnitudes is said to have the same ratio to the second, as the third has to the fourth, when any equimultiples whatsoever of the first and third being taken, and any equimultiples whatsoever of the second and fourth being taken; if the multiple of the first be less than that of the second, the multiple of the third is also less than that of the fourth: and, if the multiple of the first be equal to that of the second, the multiple of the third is also equal to that of the fourth: and, if the multiple of the first be greater than that of the second, the multiple of the third is also greater than that of the fourth.**

The statement of the above Test in symbols has already been given in Art. 35.

**Art. 68.** A particular case of the conditions is often useful.

Those conditions must hold for all integral values of $r$ and $s$.

Therefore they hold when $r = s = 1$.

* Euclid uses the term "homologous."

Hence if $A : B = C : D,$

the conditions include the following:—

(i) If $A > B$, then must $C > D$.

(ii) If $A = B$, then must $C = D$.

(iii) If $A < B$, then must $C < D$.

To (i) correspond the figures

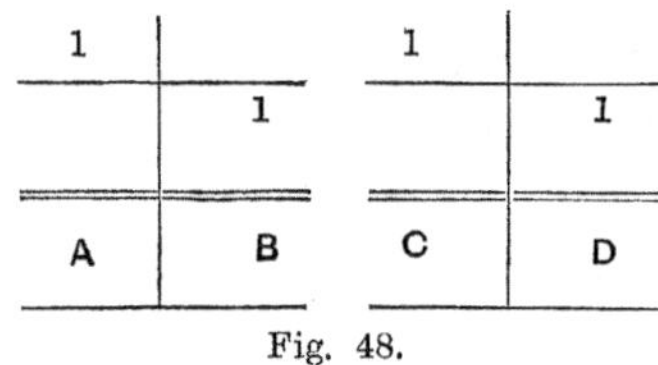


Fig. 48.

To (ii) correspond the figures

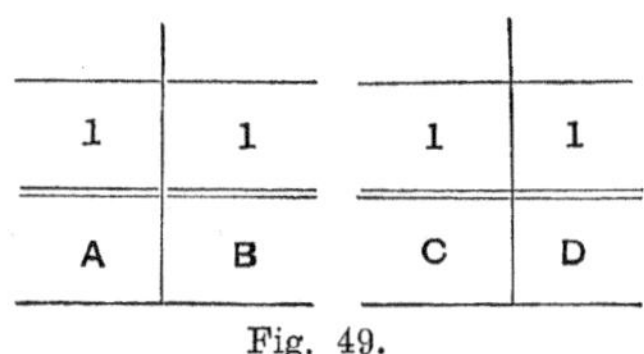


Fig. 49.

To (iii) correspond the figures

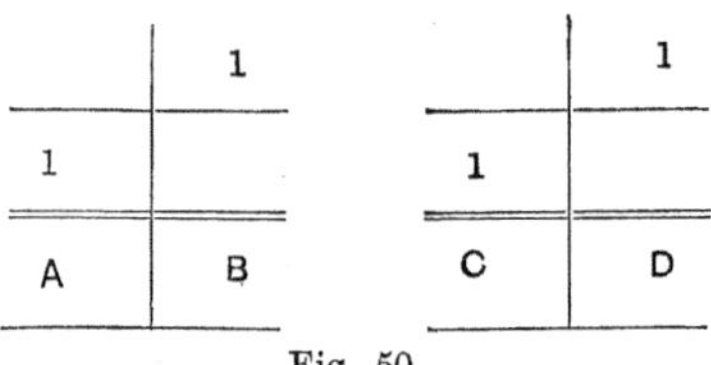


Fig. 50.

### Art. 69. *Def.* 14. THE RATIO OF EQUALITY.

**When the two terms of a ratio are equal, it is called a ratio of equality.**

### Art. 70. EXAMPLE 19.

Apply Euclid's Test for Equal Ratios to show that all ratios of equality are the same.

# SECTION IV.

## THE SIMPLER PROPOSITIONS IN THE THEORY OF RELATIVE MULTIPLE SCALES WITH GEOMETRICAL APPLICATIONS. SECOND SERIES. Nos. 17–24.

### Art. 71. PROPOSITION XVII. (Euc. VI. 1.)

Enunciation 1. The areas of parallelograms (or triangles) having the same altitude are proportional to the lengths of their bases.

Enunciation 2. *The scale of the areas of two parallelograms (or triangles) which have the same altitude is the same as that of the lengths of their bases.*

Any two parallelograms which have the same altitude may be placed so as to lie between the same parallels.

Let $ABCD$, $EFGH$, Fig. 51, be two parallelograms lying between the same parallels.

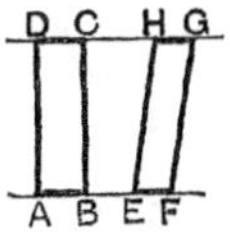

Fig. 51.

It is required to prove that

$$[AB, EF] \simeq [ABCD, EFGH].$$

Take any integer $r$ in the first column, and any integer $s$ in the second column of the scale of $AB$, $EF$.

Then there are three alternatives shown by the figures

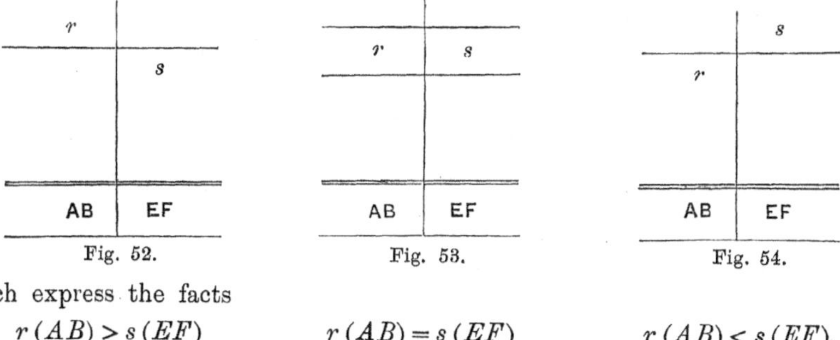


Fig. 52. Fig. 53. Fig. 54.

which express the facts

$r(AB) > s(EF)$ $\qquad$ $r(AB) = s(EF)$ $\qquad$ $r(AB) < s(EF)$.

Then in order that the scale of $AB$, $EF$ may be the same as that of $ABCD$, $EFGH$ it is necessary to show that in these several cases

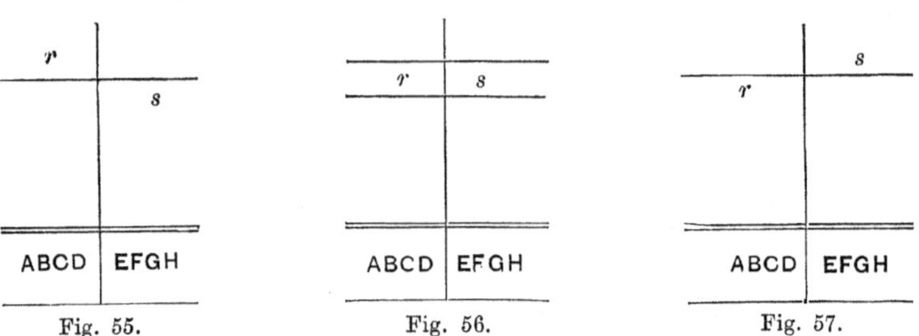


Fig. 55. Fig. 56. Fig. 57.

which express the facts

$r(ABCD) > s(EFGH)$ $r(ABCD) = s(EFGH)$ $r(ABCD) < s(EFGH)$.

On $BA$ produced set off a length $BK$ equal to $r(BA)$.

Then draw $KL$ parallel to $BC$ cutting $CD$ produced at $L$.

Then it is known by Art. 19 that $BKLC = r(ABCD)$.

On $EF$ produced set off a length $EM$ equal to $s(EF)$.

Then draw $MN$ parallel to $EH$ cutting $HG$ produced at $N$.

Then it is known by Art. 19 that $EMNH = s(EFGH)$.

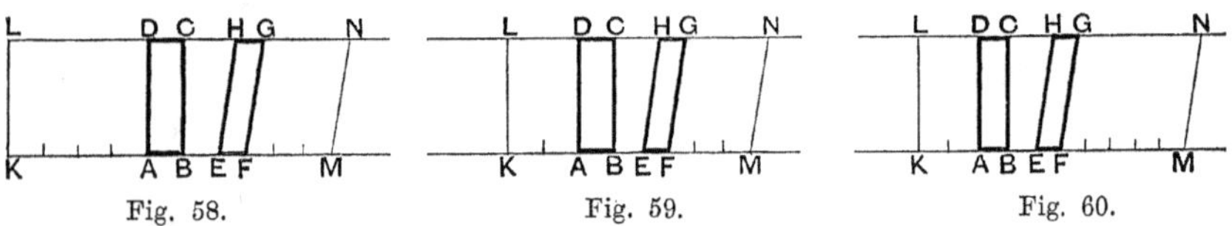


Fig. 58. Fig. 59. Fig. 60.

Hence in the several figures

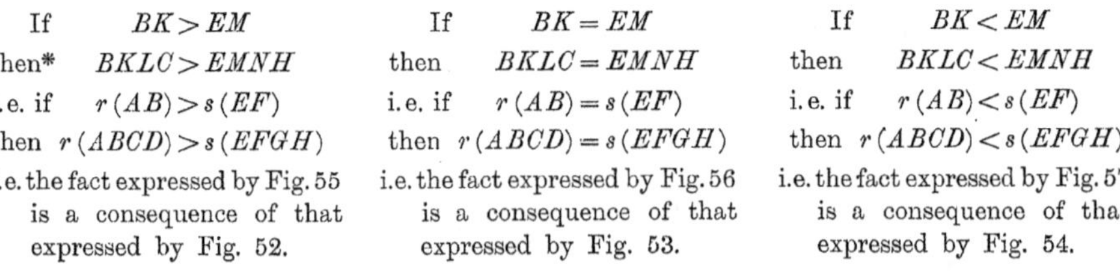

If $BK > EM$
then* $BKLC > EMNH$
i.e. if $r(AB) > s(EF)$
then $r(ABCD) > s(EFGH)$
i.e. the fact expressed by Fig. 55 is a consequence of that expressed by Fig. 52.

If $BK = EM$
then $BKLC = EMNH$
i.e. if $r(AB) = s(EF)$
then $r(ABCD) = s(EFGH)$
i.e. the fact expressed by Fig. 56 is a consequence of that expressed by Fig. 53.

If $BK < EM$
then $BKLC < EMNH$
i.e. if $r(AB) < s(EF)$
then $r(ABCD) < s(EFGH)$
i.e. the fact expressed by Fig. 57 is a consequence of that expressed by Fig. 54.

Hence the scale of $AB$, $EF$ is the same as that of $ABCD$, $EFGH$.

---

* This follows immediately from the proposition that parallelograms between the same parallels and on equal bases are equal in area.

The proof of the proposition for triangles instead of parallelograms is effected in a similar manner, the equimultiples of the triangles and their bases being constructed as in Art. 20.

## Art. 72. EXAMPLES.

**20.** Given two rectilineal areas, and a straight line, find another straight line such that the scale of the areas is the same as that of the lines.

**21.** Given two straight lines, and a rectilineal area, find another rectilineal area such that the scale of the lines is the same as that of the areas.

**22.** Given three rectilineal areas, find a fourth such that the scale of the first and second area is the same as that of the third and fourth.

**23.** Prove that the scale of the areas of two triangles on equal bases is the same as the scale of their altitudes.

**24.** If $ABC$ be a triangle, and $O$ any point in its plane, and if $AO$ cut $BC$ at $D$, prove that

$$BD : DC = \triangle AOB : \triangle AOC.$$

## Art. 73. PROPOSITION XVIII. (Euc. VI. 33.)

ENUNCIATION 1. In the same circle or in equal circles

(i) angles at the centre are proportional to the arcs on which they stand.

(ii) angles at the circumference are proportional to the arcs on which they stand.

(iii) angles at the centre are proportional to the sectors bounded by the sides of the angles and the arcs on which they stand.

ENUNCIATION 2. *In the same circle or in equal circles*

(i) *the scale of two angles at the centre is the same as that of the arcs on which they stand.*

(ii) *the scale of two angles at the circumference is the same as that of the arcs on which they stand.*

(iii) *the scale of two angles at the centre is the same as that of the sectors bounded by the sides of the angles and the arcs on which they stand.*

If the angles are in the same circle, the figure may be drawn twice over, so that it is sufficient to consider the case where there are two equal circles.

(i) Let $A$, $B$, Figs. 67—72, be the centres of two equal circles.

Let $CAD$, $EBF$ be two angles at the centres standing on the arcs $CD$, $EF$.

It is required to prove that

$$[C\hat{A}D,\ E\hat{B}F] \simeq [\text{arc } CD,\ \text{arc } EF].$$

Take any integer $r$ in the first column and any integer $s$ in the second column of the scale of $C\hat{A}D$, $E\hat{B}F$.

Then there are three alternatives shown by the figures:—

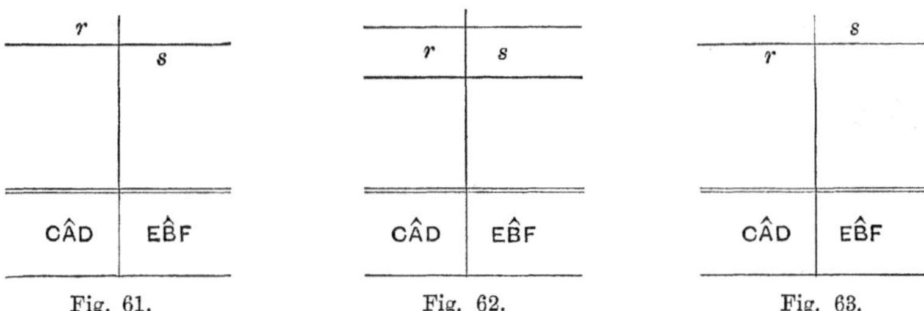


Fig. 61. Fig. 62. Fig. 63.

which express the facts

$r\,(C\hat{A}D) > s\,(E\hat{B}F)$ $r\,(C\hat{A}D) = s\,(E\hat{B}F)$ $r\,(C\hat{A}D) < s\,(E\hat{B}F)$.

Then in order that the scale of $C\hat{A}D$, $E\hat{B}F$ may be the same as the scale of arc $CD$, arc $EF$, it is necessary to show that in these several cases

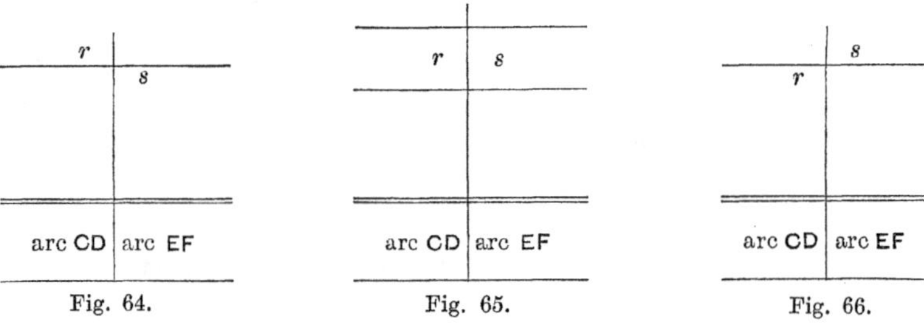


Fig. 64. Fig. 65. Fig. 66.

which express the facts

$r\,(\text{arc } CD) > s\,(\text{arc } EF)$ $r\,(\text{arc } CD) = s\,(\text{arc } EF)$ $r\,(\text{arc } CD) < s\,(\text{arc } EF)$.

Now make an angle $CAG$ equal to $r\,(C\hat{A}D)$.

Then it is known by Art. 21 that the arc $CG$ is equal to $r\,(\text{arc } CD)$.

Next make the angle $EBH$ equal to $s\,(E\hat{B}F)$.

Then it is known by Art. 21 that the arc $EH$ is equal to $s$ (arc $EF$).

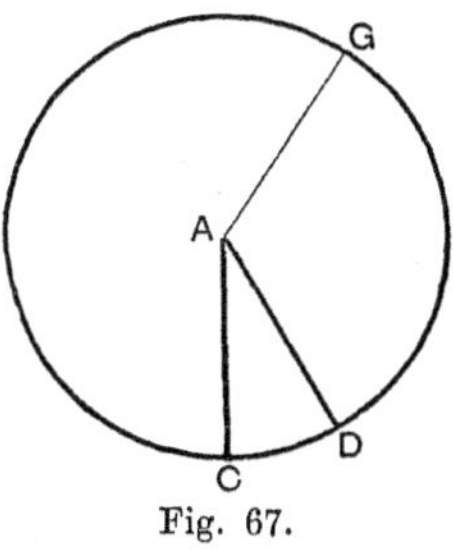

Fig. 67.

Fig. 68.

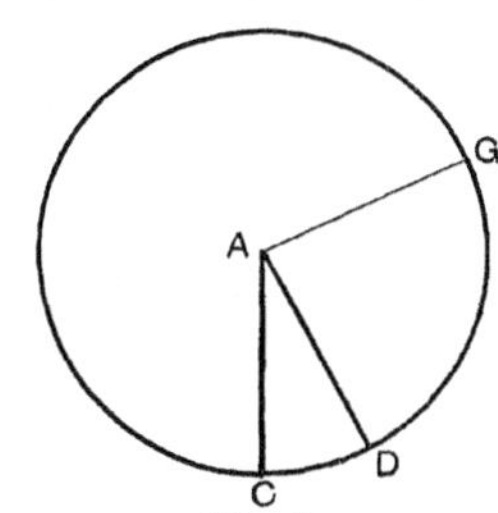

Fig. 69.

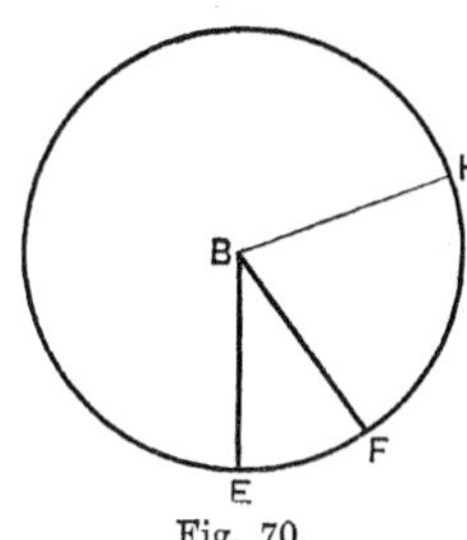

Fig. 70.

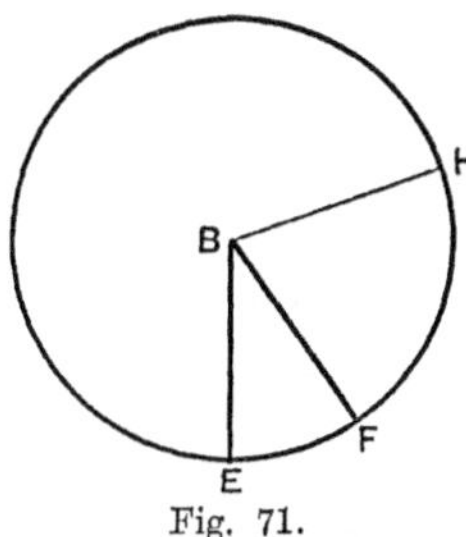

Fig. 71.

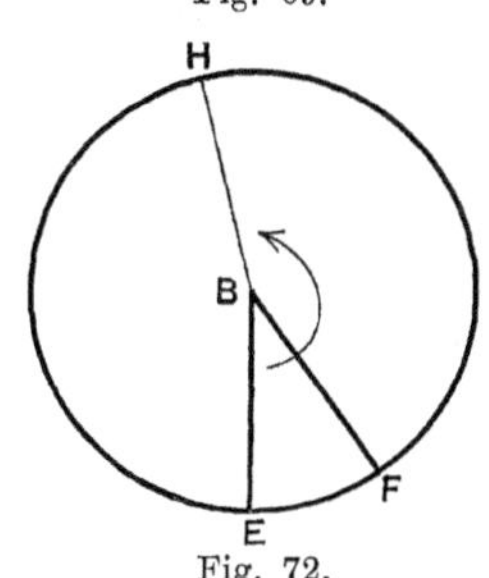

Fig. 72.

Hence in the several figures

| | | |
|---|---|---|
| If $C\hat{A}G > E\hat{B}H$ | If $C\hat{A}G = E\hat{B}H$ | If $C\hat{A}G < E\hat{B}H$ |
| then* arc $CG >$ arc $EH$ | then arc $CG =$ arc $EH$ | then arc $CG <$ arc $EH$ |
| i.e. if $r(C\hat{A}D) > s(E\hat{B}F)$ | i.e. if $r(C\hat{A}D) = s(E\hat{B}F)$ | i.e. if $r(C\hat{A}D) < s(E\hat{B}F)$ |
| then $r$ (arc $CD$) $> s$ (arc $EF$) | then $r$ (arc $CD$) $= s$ (arc $EF$) | then $r$ (arc $CD$) $< s$ (arc $EF$) |
| i.e. the fact expressed by Fig. 64 is a consequence of that expressed by Fig. 61. | i.e. the fact expressed by Fig. 65 is a consequence of that expressed by Fig. 62. | i.e. the fact expressed by Fig. 66 is a consequence of that expressed by Fig. 63. |

Hence the scale of $C\hat{A}D$, $E\hat{B}F$ is the same as that of arc $CD$, arc $EF$.

(ii) An angle at the centre of a circle is double the angle at the circumference standing on the same arc.

Hence the scale of two angles at the centre of the same or of equal circles is the same as that of the angles at the circumference on the same arcs. [Art. 42.

Hence, by case (i), the scale of two angles at the circumference of the same or of equal circles is the same as that of the arcs on which they stand. [Prop. 10.

(iii) The proof of this is derivable from that of (i) by replacing therein each arc by the corresponding sector.

* This follows immediately from the proposition that in equal circles equal angles at the centres stand on equal arcs.

### Art. 74. *Def.* 15. RECIPROCAL SCALES.

**The scale of $B$, $A$ is called the reciprocal of the scale of $A$, $B$.**

### Art. 75. EXAMPLE 25.

If two reciprocal scales are the same, prove that each must be the identical scale.

### Art. 76. *Def.* 16. RECIPROCAL RATIOS.

**The ratios $A:B$ and $B:A$ are called reciprocal ratios.**

### Art. 77. EXAMPLE 26.

If two reciprocal ratios are equal, prove that each of them is a ratio of equality.

## Art. 78. PROPOSITION XIX. (Corollary to Euc. V. 4.)*

ENUNCIATION 1. If two ratios are equal their reciprocal ratios are equal,

i.e. if $A:B=C:D$,

to prove that $B:A=D:C$.

ENUNCIATION 2. *If the scale of $A$, $B$ is the same as that of $C$, $D$, then the scale of $B$, $A$ is the same as that of $D$, $C$,*

*i.e. if* $[A, B] \simeq [C, D]$,

*then* $[B, A] \simeq [D, C]$.

Let the scale of $A$, $B$ be formed.

Let the 1st and 2nd columns be interchanged.

Then the result will be the scale of $B$, $A$.

For it is the scale which would have been formed, if after the multiples of $A$ and those of $B$ had been arranged in a vertical line in a single series in ascending order of magnitude, the multiples of $A$ had been moved to the right instead of the left as in Art. 30.

Since the original scale was also the scale of $C$, $D$, it follows that after the interchange of the 1st and 2nd columns the new scale is that of $D$, $C$.

Hence the new scale is the scale of $B$, $A$ and also that of $D$, $C$.

$$\therefore [B, A] \simeq [D, C].$$

* Simson numbers this proposition Euc. V. B.

### Art. 79. PROPOSITION XX. (i). (Euc. V. 7, 1st Part.)

ENUNCIATION 1. Equal magnitudes have the same ratio to the same magnitude,

i.e. if $A$, $B$, $C$ be three magnitudes of the same kind, and if $A$ be equal to $B$, then $$A : C = B : C.$$

ENUNCIATION 2. *If $A$, $B$, $C$ be three magnitudes of the same kind, and if $A$ be equal to $B$, then the scale of $A$, $C$ is the same as that of $B$, $C$,*

$$i.e.\ [A, C] \simeq [B, C].$$

Since $$A = B,$$

$$rA = rB,$$

$$\therefore \text{ if } rA > sC, \text{ then } rB > sC;$$

$$\text{if } rA = sC, \text{ then } rB = sC;$$

$$\text{if } rA < sC, \text{ then } rB < sC.$$

$$\therefore [A, C] \simeq [B, C].$$

### Art. 80. PROPOSITION XX. (ii). (Euc. V. 7, 2nd Part.)

ENUNCIATION 1. The same magnitude has the same ratio to equal magnitudes,

i.e. if $A$, $B$, $C$ be three magnitudes of the same kind, and if $A$ be equal to $B$, then $$C : A = C : B.$$

ENUNCIATION 2. *If $A$, $B$, $C$ be three magnitudes of the same kind, and if $A$ be equal to $B$, then the scale of $C$, $A$ is the same as that of $C$, $B$,*

$$i.e.\ [C, A] \simeq [C, B].$$

It was proved that if $A = B$,

then $$[A, C] \simeq [B, C].$$ [Prop. 20 (i).

$$\therefore [C, A] \simeq [C, B].$$ [Prop. 19.

### Art. 81. PROPOSITION XXI. (Euc. V. 9.)

ENUNCIATION 1. If $A : C = B : C$,
or if $C : A = C : B$,
to prove that $A = B$.

ENUNCIATION 2. *If the scale of A, C is the same as that of B, C; or if the scale of C, A is the same as that of C, B; then must* $A = B$.

If $[C, A] \simeq [C, B]$,
then $[A, C] \simeq [B, C]$. [Prop. 19.

Now either $A$ is equal to $B$ or not.

If $A$ is not equal to $B$,
then $[A, C]$ is not the same as $[B, C]$. [Prop. 12.

This is contrary to the hypothesis.

Hence $A$ must be equal to $B$.

### Art. 82. EXAMPLE 27.

(i) If $[rA, B] \simeq [sA, C]$, prove that $sB = rC$.

(ii) If $[A, rC] \simeq [B, sC]$, prove that $sA = rB$.

### Art. 83. PROPOSITION XXII.* (Euc. V. 16.)

ENUNCIATION 1. If $A, B, C, D$ be four magnitudes of the same kind, and if $A : B = C : D$, to prove that $A : C = B : D$.

ENUNCIATION 2. *If A, B, C, D be four magnitudes of the same kind, and if the scale of A, B be the same as that of C, D; to prove that the scale of A, C is the same as that of B, D.*

i.e. if $[A, B] \simeq [C, D]$,
then $[A, C] \simeq [B, D]$.

In proving this proposition it is convenient to use the second form of the conditions for the sameness of two scales in Prop. 8.

* See Note 6.

Take any integer $r$ in the first column, and any integer $s$ in the second column, of the scales *which are to be proved the same.*

It is necessary to show that

(1) If $rA > sC$, then $rB > sD$;

(2) If $rA < sC$, then $rB < sD$;

(3) If $rB > sD$, then $rA > sC$;

(4) If $rB < sD$, then $rA < sC$.

If
$$rA > sC,$$
then by Prop. 7 integers $n$ and $t$ exist such that
$$nrA > tB > nsC.$$

Since
$$nrA > tB,$$
the scale of $A$, $B$ shows the fact exhibited in Fig. 73.

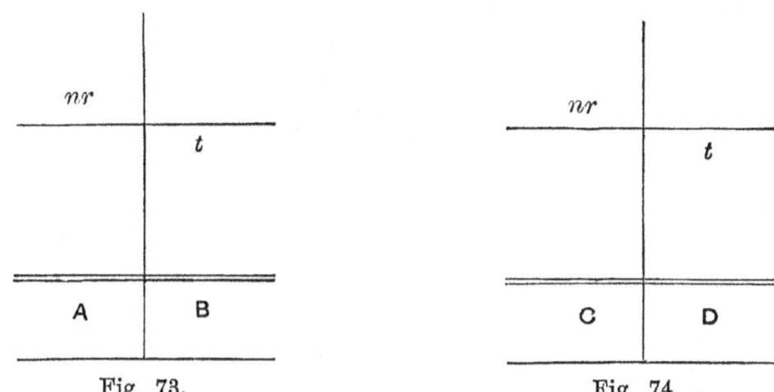


Fig. 73. Fig. 74.

But
$$[A, B] \simeq [C, D].$$

Hence the scale of $C$, $D$ shows the fact exhibited in Fig. 74.
$$\therefore\ nrC > tD. \qquad \text{(I)}$$

Now it has been shown that
$$tB > nsC. \qquad \text{(II)}$$

From (I)
$$snrC > stD.$$

From (II)
$$rtB > rnsC,$$

but
$$snrC = rnsC,$$
$$\therefore\ rtB > stD,$$
$$\therefore\ rB > sD^*.$$

* This result is an algebraic consequence of (I) and (II). It is obtained by transforming the two inequalities so that the multiple of $C$ (which is the magnitude appearing in both) becomes the same in each.

Hence if $rA > sC$, then $rB > sD$. (III)

In like* manner if $rA < sC$, then $rB < sD$; (IV)

if $rB > sD$, then $rA > sC$; (V)

if $rB < sD$, then $rA < sC$. (VI)

From (III), (IV), (V), (VI) it follows by Prop. 8 (ii) that

$$[A, C] \simeq [B, D].$$

**Art. 84.** COROLLARY. (Euc. V. 14.)

*If $A$, $B$, $C$, $D$ are all magnitudes of the same kind, and if*

$$A : B = C : D,$$

*then $A \gtreqless C$, according as $B \gtreqless D$, and conversely.*

Since $[A, B] \simeq [C, D]$,

$\therefore$ $[A, C] \simeq [B, D]$. [Prop. 22.

Suppose that $B > D$,

then the scale of $B$, $D$ shows the entry in Fig. 75.

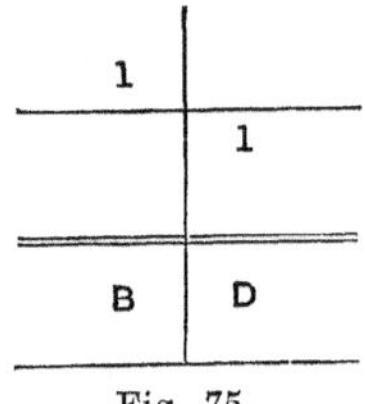

Fig. 75.

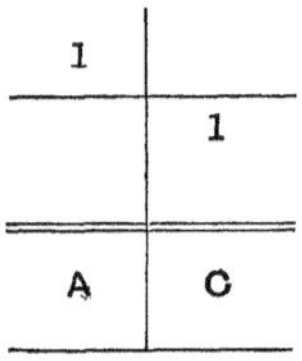

Fig. 76.

But $[A, C] \simeq [B, D]$.

Hence the scale of $A$, $C$ shows the entry in Fig. 76.

$\therefore$ $A > C$.

In a similar way, if $B = D$, it follows that $A = C$, and if $B < D$, then $A < C$.

The converse theorem may be proved in the same way or deduced from the above.

* Making the corresponding changes in the figures, the proof of (IV) is obtained from that of (III) by reversing all the signs of inequality; that of (V) is obtained from that of (III) by interchanging $A$ with $B$, $C$ with $D$; that of (VI) is obtained from that of (V) by reversing all the signs of inequality.

### Art. 85. EXAMPLES.

28. If $A : B = C : D$,

if $E : C = F : A$,

if $E : D = F : G$,

and if the magnitudes $A$, $B$, $C$, $D$, $E$, $F$, $G$ are all of the same kind, prove that $B = G$.

[The proposition is also true if $A$, $B$, $F$, $G$ are of the same kind, and if $C$, $D$, $E$ are of the same kind, as may be proved by using Prop. 35 below.]

29. If $A$, $B$, $C$, $D$ are four points on a straight line such that $B$ divides $AC$ internally in the same ratio as $D$ divides it externally; prove that $C$ divides $BD$ internally in the same ratio as $A$ divides it externally.

### Art. 86. *Def.* 17. HARMONIC POINTS.

**Four points $A$, $B$, $C$, $D$ on a straight line are said to be four harmonic points if $B$ and $D$ divide $AC$ in the same ratio, one internally and the other externally.**

Then $A$ and $C$ are called conjugate points; as are also $B$ and $D$.

### Art. 87. PROPOSITION XXIII. (Euc. VI. 2, 2nd Part.)

ENUNCIATION 1. If two sides of a triangle are divided proportionally so that the segments terminating at the vertex common to the two sides correspond to each other, then the straight line joining the points of division is parallel to the other side.

ENUNCIATION 2. *If two sides of a triangle are divided so that the scale of the segments of one side is the same as the scale of the segments of the other side, the segments terminating at the vertex common to the two sides being both the first (or both the second) terms of the scales, then the straight line joining the points of division is parallel to the other side.*

Let the points $D$ and $E$ divide the sides $AB$, $AC$ of the triangle $ABC$, so that

$$[AD, DB] \simeq [AE, EC],$$

then will $DE$ be parallel to $BC$.

If $DE$ be not parallel to $BC$, draw $BF$ parallel to $DE$ cutting $AC$ at $F$.

Then $[AD, DB] \simeq [AE, EF]$, [Prop. 13.

$\therefore$ $[AE, EC] \simeq [AE, EF]$, [Prop. 10.

$\therefore$ $EC = EF$, [Prop. 21.

which is impossible.

Hence $DE$ is parallel to $BC$.

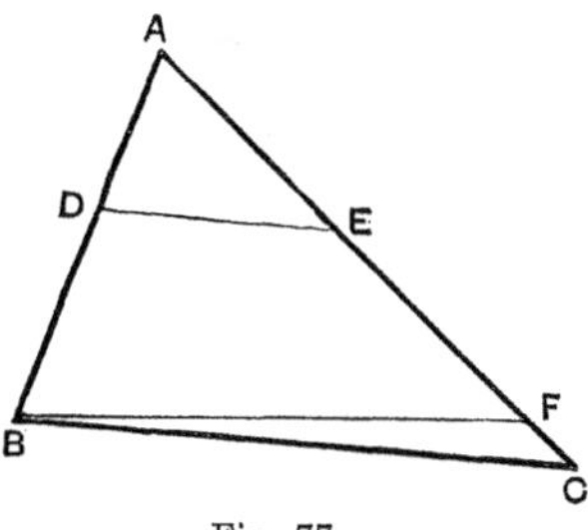

Fig. 77.

## Art. 88. EXAMPLE 30.

If $ABCD$ be a plane quadrilateral, and if $E$, $F$, $G$, $H$ be points on $AB$, $BC$, $CD$, $DA$ respectively such that

$$AE : AB = CF : CB = CG : CD = AH : AD,$$

prove that $EFGH$ is a parallelogram.

## Art. 89. PROPOSITION XXIV.*

ENUNCIATION 1. (1) A given segment of a straight line can be divided *internally* into segments having the ratio of one given line to another in one way only.

(2) A given segment of a straight line can be divided *externally* into segments having the ratio of one given line to any other not equal to it in one way only.

ENUNCIATION 2. (1) *A given segment of a straight line can be divided* internally *into segments whose scale is the same as that of two given straight lines in one way only.*

(2) *A given segment of a straight line can be divided* externally *into segments whose scale is the same as that of two given unequal straight lines in one way only.*

(1) Let $AB$ be the straight line to be divided internally at some point $C$, so that

$$[AC, CB] \simeq [K, L],$$

where $K$, $L$ are two given segments of straight lines.

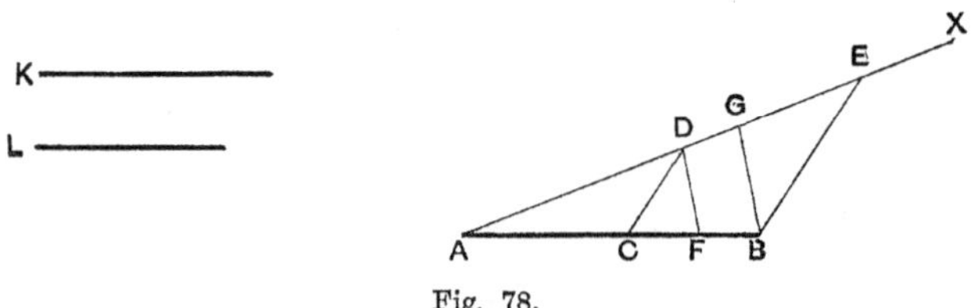

Fig. 78.

Through $A$, one of the extremities of $AB$, draw any straight line $AX$, and measure off $AD$ equal to $K$, and $DE$ equal to $L$ in the *same* direction as $AD$.

* See Note 7.

Join $BE$, and through $D$ draw $DC$ parallel to $EB$, cutting $AB$ at $C$. Then $C$ will divide $AB$, so that $[AC, CB] \simeq [K, L]$.

Since $AB$, $AX$ are cut by the parallel lines $CD$, $BE$; the segments $AC$, $CB$ correspond respectively to $AD$, $DE$.

$$\therefore\ [AC, CB] \simeq [AD, DE] \qquad \text{[Prop. 13.}$$
$$\simeq [K, L].$$

Hence $C$ is one point which satisfies the required condition.

If possible let $F$ be some other point which also satisfies the required condition.

Join $FD$, and draw $BG$ parallel to $FD$ cutting $AE$ at $G$.

Then the segments $AF$, $FB$ correspond to $AD$, $DG$ respectively.

$$\therefore\ [AF, FB] \simeq [AD, DG], \qquad \text{[Prop. 13.}$$

but by hypothesis $\quad [AF, FB] \simeq [K, L].$

$$\therefore\ [AD, DG] \simeq [K, L] \qquad \text{[Prop. 10.}$$
$$\simeq [AD, DE].$$
$$\therefore\ DG = DE \qquad \text{[Prop. 21.}$$

which is impossible.

Hence $C$ is the only point which satisfies the required condition.

It is important to notice that if $K < L$, then $AC < CB$, and $C$ is nearer to $A$ than to $B$.

If $K = L$, then $AC = CB$, and $C$ is the middle point of $AB$.

If $K > L$, then $AC > CB$, and $C$ is further from $A$ than from $B$.

These three cases correspond to different figures in the second part of the proposition.

(2) In this case the figures differ from that of the first case in having the length $DE$ (equal to $L$) measured in the *opposite* direction to $AD$; and this is the only difference in the *constructions* for the cases $K < L$, $K > L$.

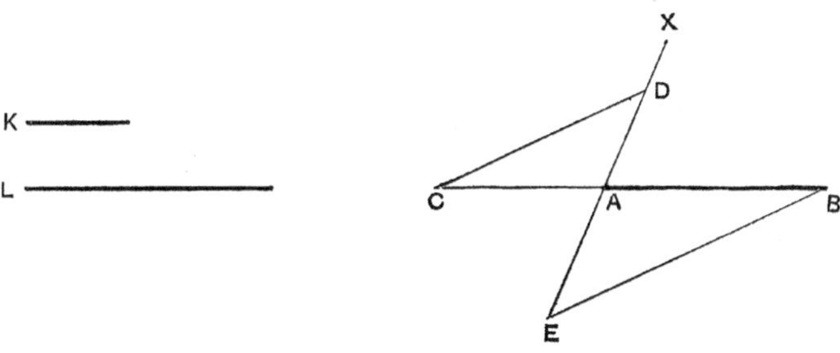


Fig. 79.

If $K < L$, then $E$ must fall on $DA$ produced through $A$ as in Fig. 79, and $C$ is nearer to $A$ than to $B$.

If $K > L$, then $E$ must fall between $D$ and $A$, as in Fig. 80, and $C$ is further from $A$ than from $B$.

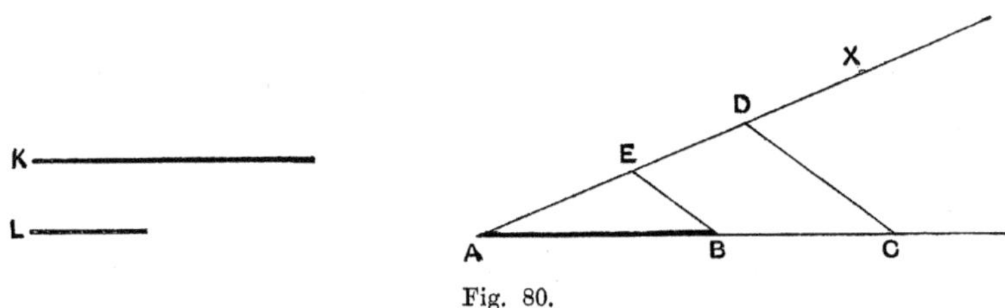

Fig. 80.

The *proofs* for the cases $K < L$ and $K > L$ are the same as in Case (1). They need not therefore be repeated.

### Art. 90. NOTE ON CASE (2) OF THE PRECEDING ARTICLE.

If $K = L$, $E$ coincides with $A$.

Hence $BE$ coincides with $BA$.

Hence the parallel through $D$ to $BE$ is parallel to $BA$.

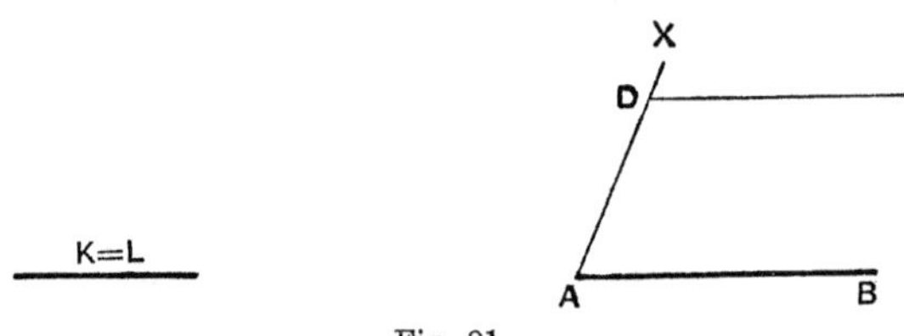

Fig. 81.

Hence in this case from Euclid's point of view the construction fails, and there is no point corresponding to $C$. See Note 7.

# SECTION V.

## SIMILAR FIGURES.

### PROPOSITIONS 25—32.

**Art. 91.** *Def.* 18.

**Similar rectilineal figures are those which satisfy the following two sets of conditions.**

**(1) The angles of one of the figures taken in order must be respectively equal to the angles of the other figure taken in order.**

**(2) Those sides in the two figures which join the vertices of equal angles being defined as corresponding sides, the ratio of any pair of corresponding sides must be equal to the ratio of every other pair of corresponding sides.**

Let $A_1B_1C_1D_1E_1$, $A_2B_2C_2D_2E_2$ be two similar figures, then the two sets of conditions are as follows:—

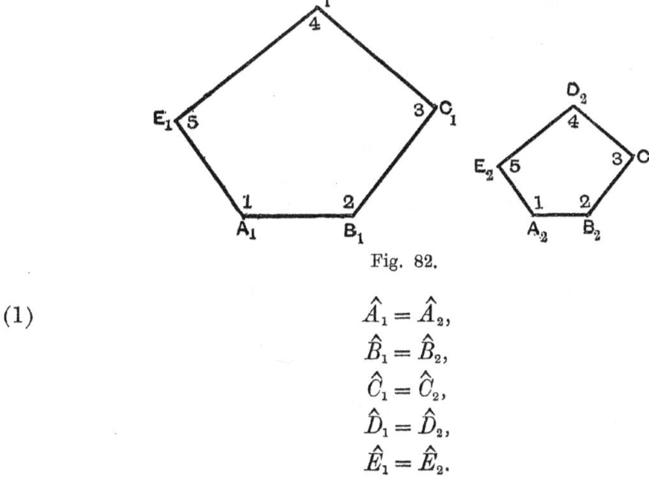


Fig. 82.

(1)

$$\hat{A}_1 = \hat{A}_2,$$
$$\hat{B}_1 = \hat{B}_2,$$
$$\hat{C}_1 = \hat{C}_2,$$
$$\hat{D}_1 = \hat{D}_2,$$
$$\hat{E}_1 = \hat{E}_2.$$

(As there is in this figure only one angle at each vertex it is sufficient to indicate each angle by the letter standing at its vertex.)

It is often convenient to indicate the equality of two angles in two similar rectilineal figures by marking the equal angles with the same number, e.g. in the above figures the equal angles at $A_1$, $A_2$ are both marked 1.

(2) Since $$\hat{A}_1 = \hat{A}_2,$$

and $$\hat{B}_1 = \hat{B}_2,$$

$\therefore$ the side $A_1B_1$ corresponds to the side $A_2B_2$.

In like manner $B_1C_1$ corresponds to $B_2C_2$, and so on.

$$\therefore\ A_1B_1 : A_2B_2 = B_1C_1 : B_2C_2 = C_1D_1 : C_2D_2 = D_1E_1 : D_2E_2 = E_1A_1 : E_2A_2.$$

**Art. 92.** *Def.* 19.

**The ratio of a side of the first figure to the corresponding side of the second figure is called the ratio of similitude of the first figure to the second.**

**Art. 93. Note.** It is obvious that two congruent figures are similar to one another. For such figures the ratio of similitude is the ratio of equality.

**Art. 94.** Similar figures are said to be *similarly described* on two straight lines, when these two straight lines are corresponding sides of the figures, e.g. :—

The figures $A_1B_1C_1D_1E_1$, $A_2B_2C_2D_2E_2$ are similarly described on $A_1B_1$, $A_2B_2$; or on $B_1C_1$, $B_2C_2$; and so on.

(In general language two similar figures are similarly described on two straight lines to which they have the same relation.)

## Art. 95. EXAMPLE 31.

If $B$ be the middle point of $AC$, and $BX$, $CY$ be drawn perpendicular to $AC$, and if $A$ be joined to any point $P$ on $BX$, and if on $AP$ on the side remote from $B$ a triangle $APQ$ be described similar to $ABP$ so that the sides $AP$, $PQ$ of $APQ$ may correspond to the sides $AB$, $BP$ of $ABP$, prove that $Q$ is equidistant from $A$ and from the straight line $CY$.

## Art. 96. PROPOSITION XXV. (Euc. VI. 21.)

ENUNCIATION. *Rectilineal figures which are similar to the same rectilineal figure are similar to one another.*

Let the figure $ABCD$ be similar to $A_1B_1C_1D_1$, and also to $A_2B_2C_2D_2$, it is required to prove that $A_1B_1C_1D_1$ and $A_2B_2C_2D_2$ are similar to each other.

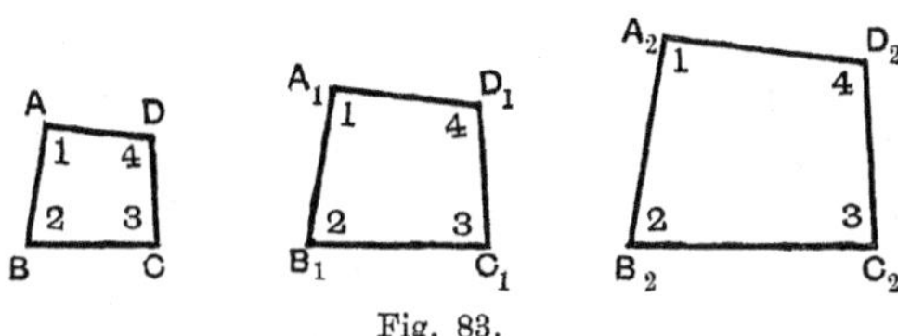


Fig. 83.

Since $ABCD$ is similar to $A_1B_1C_1D_1$

$$\therefore\ \hat{A} = \hat{A}_1,\ \hat{B} = \hat{B}_1,\ \hat{C} = \hat{C}_1,\ \hat{D} = \hat{D}_1 \ldots\ldots\ldots\ldots(1)$$

$$AB : A_1B_1 = BC : B_1C_1 = CD : C_1D_1 = DA : D_1A_1 \ \ldots\ldots\ldots(2).$$

Since $ABCD$ is similar to $A_2B_2C_2D_2$

$$\therefore\ \hat{A} = \hat{A}_2,\ \hat{B} = \hat{B}_2,\ \hat{C} = \hat{C}_2,\ \hat{D} = \hat{D}_2 \ldots\ldots\ldots\ldots(3)$$

$$AB : A_2B_2 = BC : B_2C_2 = CD : C_2D_2 = DA : D_2A_2 \ \ldots\ldots\ldots(4).$$

From (1) and (3) it follows that

$$\hat{A}_1 = \hat{A}_2,\ \hat{B}_1 = \hat{B}_2,\ \hat{C}_1 = \hat{C}_2,\ \hat{D}_1 = \hat{D}_2 \ \ldots\ldots\ldots\ldots(5).$$

From (2) $\qquad AB : A_1B_1 = BC : B_1C_1,$

$$\therefore\ AB : BC = A_1B_1 : B_1C_1. \qquad \text{[Prop. 22.}$$

Similarly from (4) $\qquad AB : BC = A_2B_2 : B_2C_2$

$$\therefore\ A_1B_1 : B_1C_1 = A_2B_2 : B_2C_2 \qquad \text{[Prop. 10.}$$

$$\therefore\ A_1B_1 : A_2B_2 = B_1C_1 : B_2C_2. \qquad \text{[Prop. 22.}$$

In like manner it can be shown that

$$B_1C_1 : B_2C_2 = C_1D_1 : C_2D_2 = D_1A_1 : D_2A_2.$$

$$\therefore\ A_1B_1 : A_2B_2 = B_1C_1 : B_2C_2 = C_1D_1 : C_2D_2 = D_1A_1 : D_2A_2 \ \ldots\ldots\ldots(6).$$

Now (5) and (6) are the two sets of conditions which must be satisfied in order that $A_1B_1C_1D_1$ and $A_2B_2C_2D_2$ may be similar (see Art. 91).

Hence $A_1B_1C_1D_1$ and $A_2B_2C_2D_2$ are similar.

## Art. 97. ON SIMILAR TRIANGLES.

The different cases, in which two triangles are similar, correspond to some extent to the cases in which two triangles are congruent.

For this reason the cases in which two triangles are congruent will first be enumerated.

**Art. 98.** *Two triangles are congruent if*

(1) The three sides of one triangle are respectively equal to the three sides of the other triangle.

(2 *a*)* Two sides and the included angle of one triangle are respectively equal to two sides and the included angle of the other triangle.

(3 *a*)† Two angles and the adjacent side of one triangle are respectively equal to two angles and the adjacent side in the other triangle.

(3 *b*)† One side, the opposite angle, and one other angle of one triangle are respectively equal to one side, the opposite angle, and one other angle in the other triangle.

Besides the above cases there should be noted the following, in which three elements (sides or angles) of one triangle are respectively equal to the three corresponding elements of the other triangle, viz. those in which

(2 *b*)* One angle, the opposite side, and one other side of one triangle are respectively equal to one angle, the opposite side and one other side of the other triangle.

In this case the angles opposite the other pair of equal sides are either equal or supplementary, and in the former alternative the triangles are congruent.

(This case is usually known as the Ambiguous Case.)

(4) Three angles of one triangle are respectively equal to three angles of the other triangle.

This last case is only mentioned in order to complete all the possible cases in which three elements of one triangle are respectively equal to the three corresponding elements of another triangle. In it the triangles are not generally congruent, but are always similar (see Prop. 26).

**Art. 99.** To case (1) above corresponds in the case of similar triangles the proposition that if the sides of one triangle taken in order are proportional to the sides of another triangle taken in order, then the triangles are similar.

* The numbers attached to the cases (2 *a*) and (2 *b*) both contain the same number 2 because in each there are two sides and one angle given equal.

† The numbers attached to the cases (3 *a*) and (3 *b*) both contain the same number 3 because in each there are two angles and one side given equal.

To case (2 *a*) corresponds the proposition that if two sides of a triangle are proportional to two sides of another triangle, and the included angles are equal, then the triangles are similar.

To case (2 *b*) corresponds the proposition that if two triangles have one angle of the one equal to one angle of the other, and the sides about one other angle proportional in such a manner that the sides opposite the equal angles correspond, then the triangles have their remaining angles either equal or supplementary, and in the former case the triangles are similar.

To cases (3 *a*), (3 *b*) and (4), in all of which the three angles of the one triangle are respectively equal to the three angles of the other triangle, corresponds the *single* proposition that if the angles of one triangle are respectively equal to the angles of another triangle, then the triangles are similar.

Hence there are four cases of similar triangles to be dealt with.

It should be noticed that the first and last amount to the proposition that, *in the case of triangles*, if either of the two sets of conditions for the similarity of rectilineal figures be satisfied, then the other set must also be satisfied.

So that the two sets of conditions for the similarity of rectilineal figures are not independent when the rectilineal figures are triangles.

**Art. 100.** In dealing with similar triangles the reader will find it useful to draw the similar triangles separately if they happen to overlap, and to mark equal angles with the same numbers, as in the figure.

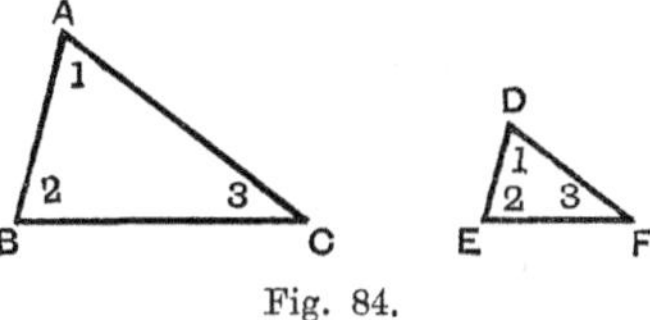


Fig. 84.

Then those sides which join the equal angles have the same numbers at their extremities, and it is therefore at once evident that they are corresponding sides.

If in the triangles $ABC$, $DEF$, $\hat{A}=\hat{D}$, $\hat{B}=\hat{E}$, and $\hat{C}=\hat{F}$, let $A$ and $D$ be marked 1, let $B$ and $E$ be marked 2, and let $C$ and $F$ be marked 3.

Write down all the possible pairs of the numbers 1, 2, 3, viz.:—23, 31, 12.

Now 2 and 3 are at the extremities of $BC$ in one triangle, and at the extremities of $EF$ in the other.

Hence $BC$, $EF$ are corresponding sides.

In like manner the positions of the numbers 3 and 1 indicate that $CA$, $DF$ are corresponding sides, and the positions of the numbers 1 and 2 indicate that $AB$ and $DE$ are corresponding sides.

$$\therefore\ BC : EF = CA : FD = AB : DE.$$

## Art. 101. PROPOSITION XXVI. (Euc. VI. 4.)

ENUNCIATION. *If the three angles of one triangle are respectively equal to the three angles of another triangle, then the triangles are similar.*

*Those sides correspond which join the vertices of equal angles.*

In the triangles $ABC$, $DEF$, let

$$\hat{A} = \hat{D},$$
$$\hat{B} = \hat{E},$$
$$\hat{C} = \hat{F}.$$

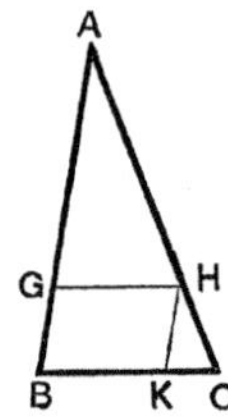

Fig. 85.

To prove that the triangles are similar*.

From $A$ on $AB$ measure off a length $AG$ equal to $DE$, and then draw $GH$ parallel to $BC$ cutting $AC$ at $H$.

It will first be shown that the triangles $AGH$, $DEF$ are congruent.

Since $GH$ is parallel to $BC$,

$$A\hat{G}H = A\hat{B}C = D\hat{E}F.$$

Also $$G\hat{A}H = B\hat{A}C = E\hat{D}F,$$

and $$AG = DE.$$

Hence the triangles $AGH$, $DEF$ are congruent.

$$\therefore\ AH = DF,$$
$$GH = EF.$$

Since $GH$ is parallel to $BC$,

$$\therefore\ BA : GA = CA : HA.$$ [Prop. 13.

$$\therefore\ BA : DE = CA : DF.$$

Now draw $HK$ parallel to $AB$.

Then $$CA : HA = CB : KB.$$ [Prop. 13.

Now $BGHK$ is a parallelogram,

$$\therefore\ BK = GH = EF$$

and $$HA = DF.$$

$$\therefore\ CA : DF = CB : EF.$$

* Observe that if the triangles are similar, the vertex $A$ of the triangle $ABC$ corresponds to the vertex $D$ of the triangle $DEF$;

and the side $AB$ of the triangle $ABC$ corresponds to the side $DE$ of the triangle $DEF$.

Hence $BA : DE = CA : DF = CB : EF$, [Prop. 10.

which, taking the letters in order, may be more conveniently written

$$AB : DE = BC : EF = CA : FD.$$

Now $AB$, $DE$ join the vertices of equal angles, and are therefore corresponding sides.

In like manner $BC$ corresponds to $EF$, and $CA$ to $FD$.

But also $\hat{A} = \hat{D}$; $\hat{B} = \hat{E}$; $\hat{C} = \hat{F}$.

Hence the two sets of conditions for the similarity of the triangles $ABC$, $DEF$ are satisfied.

Hence the triangles are similar.

## Art. 102. NOTE.

It may be noticed that corresponding sides of the triangles are opposite to equal angles; e.g. $AB$ corresponds to $DE$, and they are opposite to the equal angles $\hat{C}$ and $\hat{F}$ respectively.

## Art. 103. COROLLARY TO PROP. 26.

*If a triangle be cut by a straight line parallel to one of the sides, the triangular portion cut off is similar to the whole triangle.*

For with the figure of Prop. 26, $GH$ may be regarded as any straight line parallel to $BC$, the triangles $AGH$, $ABC$ are equiangular, and therefore similar by Prop. 26.

## Art. 104. EXAMPLES.

**32.** Show how to draw a straight line across two of the sides of a triangle, but not parallel to the third side, which will cut off a triangle similar to the original triangle.

When will it be impossible to do this?

**33.** If $ABC$ be a triangle inscribed in a circle, and $CD$ a diameter of the circle, and $AE$ a perpendicular from $A$ on the side $BC$, show that the triangles $AEB$, $ACD$ are similar.

## Art. 105. PROPOSITION XXVII.* (Euc. VI. 5.)

ENUNCIATION. *If the sides* taken in order *of one triangle are proportional to the sides* taken in order *of another triangle, prove that the triangles are similar, and that those angles are equal which are opposite to corresponding sides.*

In the triangles $ABC$, $DEF$ let it be given that

$$AB : DE = BC : EF = CA : FD, \qquad \text{(I)}$$

to prove that the triangles $ABC$, $DEF$ are similar.

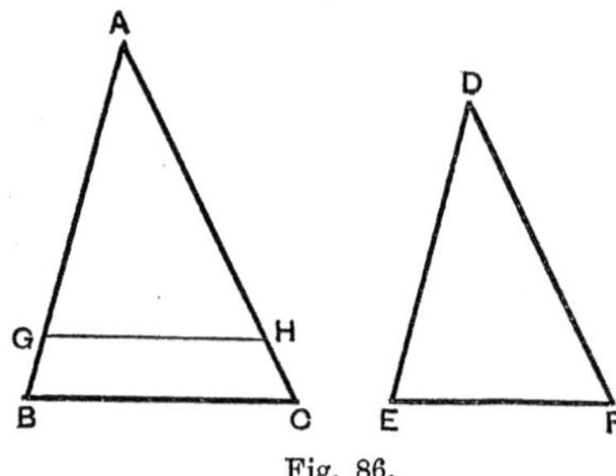


Fig. 86.

From $A$ the vertex of the triangle $ABC$ which corresponds to $D$, measure off on $AB$, the side corresponding to $DE$, a length $AG$ equal to $DE$.

Draw $GH$ parallel to $BC$, cutting $AC$ at $H$.

It will first be shown that the triangles $AGH$ and $DEF$ are congruent.

The triangles $AGH$ and $ABC$ have the angles of the one respectively equal to the angles of the other.

Therefore by Prop. 26 they are similar.

$$\therefore\ AB : AG = BC : GH = CA : HA. \qquad \text{(II)}$$

Now $DE = AG$,

$$\therefore\ AB : DE = AB : AG.$$ [Prop. 20 (ii).

Hence each of the three ratios marked (I) is equal to each of the three ratios marked (II).

$$\therefore\ BC : EF = BC : GH,$$

$$\therefore\ EF = GH.$$ [Prop. 21.

* See Note 8.

Also $$CA : FD = CA : HA,$$
$$\therefore\ FD = HA. \qquad \text{[Prop. 21.}$$

Hence in the triangles $DEF$, $AGH$,
$$DE = AG,$$
$$EF = GH,$$
$$FD = HA;$$
$\therefore$ they are congruent.
$$\therefore\ E\hat{D}F = G\hat{A}H = B\hat{A}C,$$
$$D\hat{E}F = A\hat{G}H = A\hat{B}C,$$
$$E\hat{F}D = A\hat{H}G = B\hat{C}A.$$

Hence in the triangles $ABC$, $DEF$
$$AB : DE = BC : EF = CA : FD,$$
$$\hat{A} = \hat{D},\quad \hat{B} = \hat{E},\quad \hat{C} = \hat{F}.$$

Hence the triangles are similar.

The equal angles $B\hat{A}C$, $E\hat{D}F$ are opposite the corresponding sides $BC$, $EF$.

The equal angles $A\hat{B}C$, $D\hat{E}F$ are opposite the corresponding sides $CA$, $FD$.

The equal angles $B\hat{C}A$, $E\hat{F}D$ are opposite the corresponding sides $AB$, $DE$.

## Art. 106. NOTE ON PROPOSITION 27.

The proviso that the sides of the triangles are proportional *when taken in order* is very important.

It is quite possible for the sides of one triangle to be proportional to the sides of another without the triangles being similar.

Suppose that in the triangles $ABC$, $DEF$,
$$BC : CA = EF : DE,$$
and
$$BC : AB = FD : DE,$$
then it may be proved (see Proposition 56 below) that
$$CA : AB = FD : FE.$$

But the triangles are not similar.

In the first proportion $BC$ corresponds to $EF$.

In the second proportion $BC$ corresponds to $FD$.

Hence the sides of the two triangles cannot be made to correspond.

## Art. 107. PROPOSITION XXVIII. (Euc. VI. 6.)

ENUNCIATION. *If two sides of one triangle be proportional to two sides of another triangle, and if the included angles be equal, then the triangles are similar; and those angles are equal which are opposite to corresponding sides.*

In the triangles $ABC$, $DEF$ let it be given that

$$BA : AC = ED : DF,$$

and

$$B\hat{A}C = E\hat{D}F,$$

it is required to prove that the triangles are similar; and that the angles $BCA$, $EFD$ opposite the corresponding sides $BA$, $ED$ are equal; and that the angles $ABC$, $DEF$ opposite the corresponding sides $AC$, $DF$ are equal.

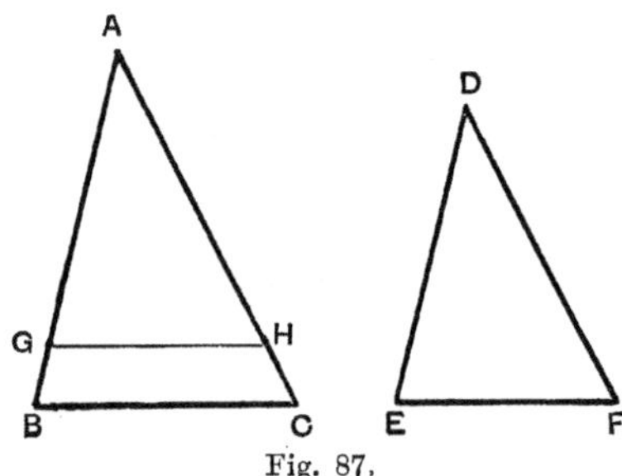

Fig. 87.

From $A$, the vertex of the triangle $ABC$ which corresponds to $D$, measure off on $AB$, the side corresponding to $DE$, a length $AG$ equal to $DE$.

Draw $GH$ parallel to $BC$ cutting $AC$ at $H$.

It will first be proved that the triangles $AGH$, $DEF$ are congruent.

Since $GH$ is parallel to $BC$,

$\therefore\ BA : GA = CA : HA,$ [Prop. 13.

$\therefore\ BA : CA = GA : HA;$ [Prop. 22.

but it is given that $BA : CA = ED : DF,$

$\therefore\ ED : DF = GA : HA.$ [Prop. 10.

But $ED = GA$ by construction,

$\therefore\ DF = HA.$ [Prop. 21.

Now in the triangles $DEF$, $AGH$,

$$DE = AG,$$
$$DF = AH,$$
$$E\hat{D}F = B\hat{A}C = G\hat{A}H.$$

Hence the triangles $DEF$, $AGH$ are congruent.

$$\therefore \; D\hat{E}F = A\hat{G}H = A\hat{B}C,$$

and
$$D\hat{F}E = A\hat{H}G = A\hat{C}B.$$

Hence the angles of the triangle $DEF$ are respectively equal to the angles of the triangle $ABC$.

Hence by Prop. 26 the triangles $DEF$, $ABC$ are similar, and those angles are equal which are opposite to corresponding sides.

## Art. 108. EXAMPLES.

**34.** Two parallel straight lines are cut by any number of straight lines passing through a fixed point.

Prove that the intercepts made on the parallel lines by any two of the straight lines through the fixed point have a constant ratio.

**35.** If the tangents at $A$ and $B$ to a circle meet at $C$, and if $P$ be any point on the circle, and if $PQ$, $PR$, $PS$ be drawn perpendicular to $AC$, $CB$, $BA$ respectively, then prove that the triangles $PAS$, $PBR$ are similar; and that the triangles $PBS$, $PAQ$ are similar; and that $PS$ is a mean proportional between $PQ$ and $PR$.

**36.*** If $C$ be the centre of a circle, $F$ any point outside it, if $FA$, $FB$ be tangents to the circle at $A$ and $B$ respectively, if $FP$ be any straight line through $F$ cutting the circle at $P$; and if through $P$ a straight line be drawn perpendicular to $FP$ cutting $CA$ at $Q$ and $CB$ at $R$; then prove that the triangles $CFQ$, $CRF$ are similar; and that $CF$ is a mean proportional between $CQ$ and $CR$.

**37.** Let $O$ be the centre of a circle, and $C$ a fixed point in its plane. Let $CO$ cut the circle at $A$ and $B$. Let $P$ be any point on the circle, and through $P$ let a straight line be drawn perpendicular to $CP$, cutting the tangents at $A$ and $B$ at $Q$ and $R$ respectively, then prove that

(1) the triangles $ACQ$, $BCR$ are similar.

(2) $AQ : AC = BC : BR$.

(3) the angle $QCR$ is a right angle.

## Art. 109. PROPOSITION XXIX. (Euc. VI. 7.)

ENUNCIATION. *If two triangles have one angle of the one equal to one angle of the other, and the sides about one other angle in each proportional in such a manner that the sides opposite to the equal angles correspond, then the triangles have their remaining angles either equal or supplementary, and in the former case the triangles are similar.*

In the triangles $ABC$, $DEF$ it is given that

$$A\hat{B}C = D\hat{E}F,$$

and $$BA : AC = ED : DF,$$

to prove that either

(1) $$A\hat{C}B = D\hat{F}E,$$

and the triangles $ABC$, $DEF$ are similar;

or (2) $$A\hat{C}B + D\hat{F}E = \text{two right angles*}.$$

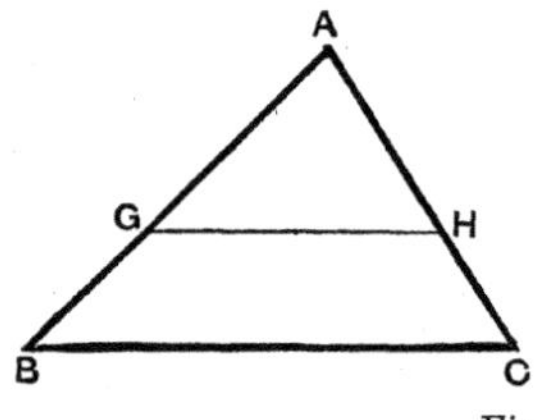


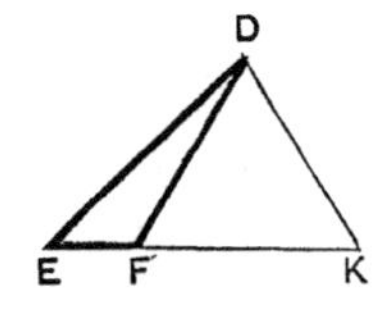


Fig. 88.

On $AB$, the side corresponding to $DE$, take a length $AG$ equal to $DE$, and draw $GH$ parallel to $BC$ cutting $AC$ at $H$.

The triangles $AGH$, $DEF$ will first be compared.

Since $GH$ is parallel to $BC$,

$$\therefore\ BA : GA = CA : HA, \qquad \text{[Prop. 13.}$$

$$\therefore\ BA : CA = GA : HA. \qquad \text{[Prop. 22.}$$

But $$BA : CA = ED : DF,$$

$$\therefore\ ED : DF = GA : HA. \qquad \text{[Prop. 10.}$$

* Notice that the sides about the angles $BAC$, $EDF$ are proportional in such a manner that the sides $AC$, $DF$ opposite the equal angles $ABC$, $DEF$ correspond.

Notice further that in each triangle two angles have been referred to, viz. $A\hat{B}C$, $B\hat{A}C$ in the triangle $ABC$ and $D\hat{E}F$, $E\hat{D}F$ in the triangle $DEF$, and therefore the remaining angles are $A\hat{C}B$, $D\hat{F}E$.

But $$AG = DE,$$

$$\therefore \; DF = HA. \qquad \text{[Prop. 21.}$$

Now in the triangles $DEF$, $AGH$,

$$DE = AG,$$
$$DF = AH,$$
$$D\hat{E}F = A\hat{B}C = A\hat{G}H,$$

where it is to be noticed that the equal angles are *opposite* to equal sides.

Now there are necessarily two alternatives,

either (1) $$G\hat{A}H = E\hat{D}F,$$

or (2) $G\hat{A}H$ is not equal to $E\hat{D}F$.

(1) If $$G\hat{A}H = E\hat{D}F,$$

then $$B\hat{A}C = E\hat{D}F,$$

and since $$A\hat{B}C = D\hat{E}F,$$

$$\therefore \; B\hat{C}A = E\hat{F}D,$$

and in this case the triangles $ABC$, $DEF$ are similar. [Prop. 26.

(2) If $G\hat{A}H$ be not equal to $E\hat{D}F$, draw $DK$, making $E\hat{D}K$ equal $B\hat{A}C$, and cutting $EF$ at $K$.

Then in the triangles $AGH$, $EDK$,

$$A\hat{G}H = A\hat{B}C = D\hat{E}K,$$
$$G\hat{A}H = E\hat{D}K,$$
$$AG = DE.$$

Hence the triangles $AGH$, $DEK$ are congruent.

$$\therefore \; AH = DK,$$
$$A\hat{H}G = D\hat{K}E.$$

But $$AH = DF,$$

$$\therefore \; DF = DK,$$
$$\therefore \; D\hat{K}F = D\hat{F}K.$$

Therefore
$$\begin{aligned} A\hat{C}B + D\hat{F}E &= A\hat{H}G + D\hat{F}E \\ &= D\hat{K}E + D\hat{F}E \\ &= D\hat{F}K + D\hat{F}E \\ &= \text{two right angles.} \end{aligned}$$

## Art. 110. NOTE.

Euclid's method of stating Proposition 29 amounts to the insertion of additional conditions in the statement here given, the effect of which is to exclude the second alternative in those cases in which the two alternatives are really distinct.

It is as follows:—

If two triangles have one angle of the one equal to one angle of the other, and the sides about two other angles proportionals; then if each of the remaining angles be either less or greater than a right angle, or if one of them be a right angle, the triangles are similar and have those angles equal about which the sides are proportionals.

Hence the additional conditions are that $A\hat{C}B$ and $D\hat{F}E$ are both less than a right angle, or both greater than a right angle, or one of them is a right angle.

If they are both less than a right angle, their sum is less than two right angles.

If they are both greater than a right angle, their sum is greater than two right angles.

In neither of these cases can the second alternative hold.

Hence the first alternative must hold, and the triangles are similar; the angles between the proportional sides being equal.

If next one of the two angles $ACB$, $DFE$ is a right angle, then, whichever alternative hold, the other angle is a right angle, hence the remaining angles are equal, and the triangles are similar.

This is the case in which the two alternatives are not really distinct.

## Art. 111. EXAMPLE 38.

If $B$ and $C$ are the centres of two circles, and $A$ the point of intersection of their internal or of their external common tangents, and if $APQ$ be any straight line through $A$ cutting the first circle at $P$ and the second at $Q$, prove that the angles $APB$, $AQC$ are either equal or supplementary.

## Art. 112. PROPOSITION XXX. (Euc. VI. 18.)

ENUNCIATION. *On a given straight line to describe a rectilineal figure similar and similarly situated to a given rectilineal figure.*

Let $A_1B_1C_1D_1E_1$ be the given rectilineal figure; it is required to describe a similar figure on the given straight line $A_2B_2$, so that $A_1B_1$ and $A_2B_2$ may be corresponding sides of the figures.

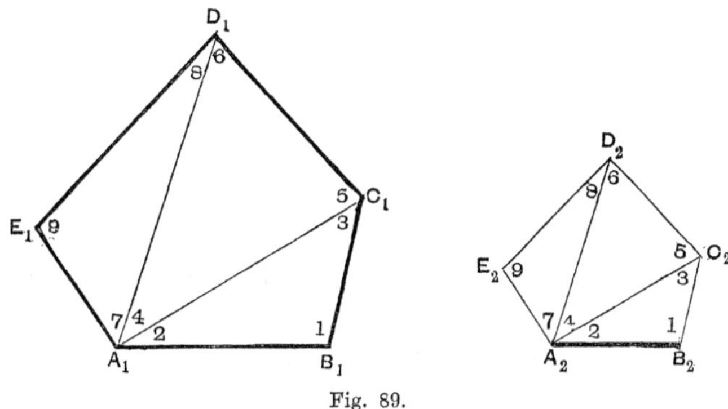


Fig. 89.

Join $A_1C_1$, $A_1D_1$.

At $B_2$ draw a straight line making with $A_2B_2$ an angle equal to $A_1\hat{B}_1C_1$, and at $A_2$ draw a straight line making with $A_2B_2$ an angle equal to $B_1A_1C_1$. Let these straight lines meet at $C_2$.

At $C_2$ draw a straight line making with $A_2C_2$ an angle equal to $A_1C_1D_1$, and at $A_2$ draw a straight line making with $A_2C_2$ an angle equal to $C_1A_1D_1$. Let these straight lines meet at $D_2$.

At $D_2$ draw a straight line making with $D_2A_2$ an angle equal to $A_1D_1E_1$, and at $A_2$ draw a straight line making with $A_2D_2$ an angle equal to $D_1A_1E_1$. Let these straight lines meet at $E_2$.

It will be proved that $A_1B_1C_1D_1E_1$ and $A_2B_2C_2D_2E_2$ are similar figures, and that $A_1B_1$ and $A_2B_2$ are corresponding sides.

In the three pairs of triangles in Figure 89, viz.:—$A_1B_1C_1$ and $A_2B_2C_2$, $A_1C_1D_1$ and $A_2C_2D_2$, $A_1D_1E_1$ and $A_2D_2E_2$, let the equal angles be marked with the same numbers. Then in each pair of triangles two angles of the one triangle are respectively equal to two angles in the other triangle. Therefore the remaining angles are equal. Let these be marked with the same number.

Then it is at once apparent that the angles at $A_1$, $B_1$, $C_1$, $D_1$, $E_1$ of the figure $A_1B_1C_1D_1E_1$ are respectively equal to the angles at $A_2$, $B_2$, $C_2$, $D_2$, $E_2$ of the figure $A_2B_2C_2D_2E_2$; so that the first set of conditions (see Art. 91) for the similarity of the two figures is satisfied.

Next the triangles $A_1B_1C_1$ and $A_2B_2C_2$ are equiangular and therefore by Prop. 26 are similar.

In like manner the triangles $A_1C_1D_1$ and $A_2C_2D_2$ are similar; and the triangles $A_1D_1E_1$ and $A_2D_2E_2$ are similar.

From these pairs of similar triangles follow the relations

$$B_1C_1 : B_2C_2 = C_1A_1 : C_2A_2 = A_1B_1 : A_2B_2 \quad \text{..................} \quad (1),$$

$$C_1A_1 : C_2A_2 = A_1D_1 : A_2D_2 = D_1C_1 : D_2C_2 \quad \text{..................} \quad (2),$$

$$A_1D_1 : A_2D_2 = D_1E_1 : D_2E_2 = E_1A_1 : E_2A_2 \quad \text{..................} \quad (3).$$

Hence by Prop. 10

$$A_1B_1 : A_2B_2 = B_1C_1 : B_2C_2 = C_1D_1 : C_2D_2 = D_1E_1 : D_2E_2 = E_1A_1 : E_2A_2.$$

Hence the second set of conditions (see Art. 91) for the similarity of the two figures is also satisfied.

Hence the two figures $A_1B_1C_1D_1E_1$ and $A_2B_2C_2D_2E_2$ are similar figures, and $A_1B_1$ and $A_2B_2$ are corresponding sides. Therefore the figures are similarly described on $A_1B_1$ and $A_2B_2$ (see Art. 94).

### Art. 113. PROPOSITION XXXI. (Included in Euc. VI. 20.)

ENUNCIATION. *Two similar rectilineal figures may be divided into the same number of triangles such that every triangle in either figure is similar to one triangle in the other figure.*

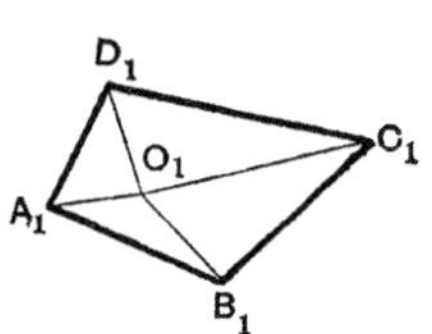


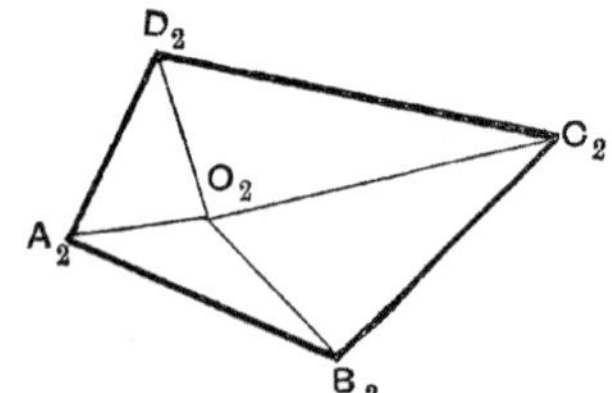


Fig. 90.

Let $A_1B_1C_1D_1$, $A_2B_2C_2D_2$ be two similar figures, such that

$$D_1\hat{A}_1B_1 = D_2\hat{A}_2B_2,$$
$$A_1\hat{B}_1C_1 = A_2\hat{B}_2C_2,$$
$$B_1\hat{C}_1D_1 = B_2\hat{C}_2D_2,$$
$$C_1\hat{D}_1A_1 = C_2\hat{D}_2A_2,$$

and $$A_1B_1 : A_2B_2 = B_1C_1 : B_2C_2 = C_1D_1 : C_2D_2 = D_1A_1 : D_2A_2.$$

Let $O_1$ be any point in the plane of $A_1B_1C_1D_1$, and join $O_1A_1$, $O_1B_1$, $O_1C_1$, $O_1D_1$.

Through $A_2$ draw a straight line making with $A_2B_2$ an angle equal to $B_1\hat{A}_1O_1$.

Through $B_2$ draw a straight line making with $B_2A_2$ an angle equal to $A_1\hat{B}_1O_1$.

Let these two straight lines meet at $O_2$.

Join $O_2C_2$, $O_2D_2$.

It will be proved that the triangles $O_1A_1B_1$, $O_2A_2B_2$ are similar; that the triangles $O_1B_1C_1$, $O_2B_2C_2$ are similar, and so on.

Since $$O_1\hat{A}_1B_1 = O_2\hat{A}_2B_2,$$
$$O_1\hat{B}_1A_1 = O_2\hat{B}_2A_2,$$
$$\therefore\ A_1\hat{O}_1B_1 = A_2\hat{O}_2B_2.$$

Hence the triangles $A_1O_1B_1$, $A_2O_2B_2$ are similar. [Prop. 26.

$$\therefore\ A_1B_1 : A_2B_2 = B_1O_1 : B_2O_2 = O_1A_1 : O_2A_2.$$

Since $$A_1B_1 : A_2B_2 = B_1C_1 : B_2C_2,$$
$$\therefore\ B_1O_1 : B_2O_2 = B_1C_1 : B_2C_2,$$
$$\therefore\ B_1O_1 : B_1C_1 = B_2O_2 : B_2C_2.$$ [Prop. 22.

Also $$A_1\hat{B}_1C_1 = A_2\hat{B}_2C_2;$$
$$A_1\hat{B}_1O_1 = A_2\hat{B}_2O_2,$$
$$\therefore\ O_1\hat{B}_1C_1 = O_2\hat{B}_2C_2.$$

Hence by Prop. 28 the triangles $O_1B_1C_1$, $O_2B_2C_2$ are similar.

In like manner the triangles $O_1C_1D_1$ and $O_2C_2D_2$ can be proved to be similar; and also $O_1D_1A_1$, $O_2D_2A_2$ can be proved to be similar.

So the two similar figures are divided up into the same number of triangles, such that every triangle in either figure is similar to one triangle in the other figure.

The point $O_1$ in the one figure corresponds to the point $O_2$ in the other figure.

Since $O_1$ is any point in the one figure, it follows that to every point in one of the figures corresponds one and only one point of the other figure.

### Art. 114. COROLLARY.

*If in Figure 90 the first figure be placed on the second so that $O_1$ falls on $O_2$, $O_1A_1$ falls along $O_2A_2$, $O_1B_1$ falls along $O_2B_2$, it can be shown that the sides of the first figure will then be parallel to and in the same direction as the corresponding sides of the second, and that the distances from $O_1$ or $O_2$ to a point on either figure along any straight line are in the ratio of similitude of the figures.*

*If $O_1$ be placed on $O_2$, $O_1A_1$ along $A_2O_2$ produced through $O_2$, and $O_1B_1$ along $B_2O_2$ produced through $O_2$, the sides of the first figure will then be parallel but in the opposite direction to the corresponding sides of the second figure.*

When the two figures have been placed as described in either of the two preceding cases, then the point $O_2$, with which $O_1$ coincides, is called a centre of similitude of the two figures.

The term centre of similitude is not however restricted to rectilineal figures. (See Art. 115, Ex. 40 below.)

### Art. 115. EXAMPLES.

**39.** If two similar rectilineal figures are placed so that two consecutive sides of one figure are respectively parallel and both in the same direction as, or both in the opposite direction to, the corresponding sides of the other figure, then each side of the one figure will be parallel to the corresponding side of the other figure, and the straight lines joining corresponding angular points of the two figures are all parallel or meet in a point; and in the latter case the distances from that point along any straight line to the points where it meets corresponding sides of the figures are in the ratio of similitude of the figures.

What is the ratio of similitude when the lines joining corresponding angular points are parallel?

**40.** If the straight line joining the centres $A$, $B$ of two circles be divided internally and externally in the ratio of the radii of the circles, (the segment of the line $AB$ terminated at $A$ corresponding to the radius of the circle whose centre is $A$), then show that the points of division may be regarded as centres of similitude of the circles.

### Art. 116. PROPOSITION XXXII. (Euc. VI. 8.)

ENUNCIATION. *If a right-angled triangle be divided into two parts by a perpendicular drawn from the vertex of the right angle on to the hypotenuse, then the triangles so formed are similar to each other and to the whole triangle; the perpendicular is a mean proportional between the segments of the hypotenuse; and each side is a mean proportional between the adjacent segment of the hypotenuse and the hypotenuse.*

If $ABC$ be the triangle, and $B$ the vertex of the right angle, and if $BD$ be drawn perpendicular to $AC$, it is required to prove

(1) that the triangles $ABC$, $ABD$, $BDC$ are similar.

(2) that $BD$ is a mean proportional between $AD$ and $DC$.

(3) that $BC$ is a mean proportional between $CD$ and $AC$.

(4) that $BA$ is a mean proportional between $AD$ and $AC$.

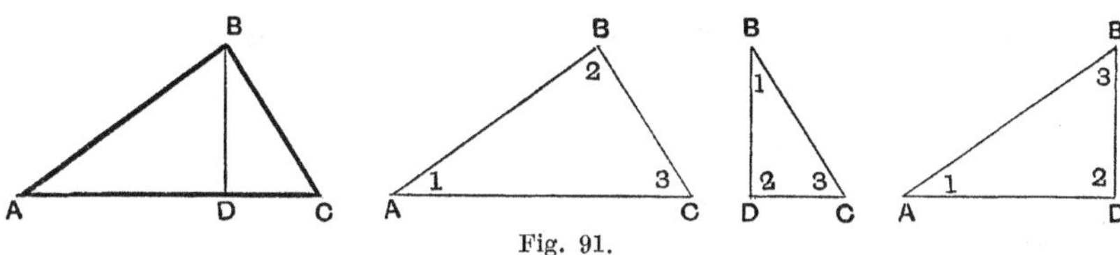


Fig. 91.

The triangles $ABC$, $ABD$ will be compared first.

$$B\hat{A}C = B\hat{A}D$$

$$A\hat{B}C = A\hat{D}B = \text{a right angle.}$$

$$\therefore\ A\hat{C}B = A\hat{B}D.$$

Hence the triangles are similar (Prop. 26).

$$\therefore\ BC : DB = CA : BA = AB : AD.$$

Since $$CA : BA = BA : AD,$$

$\therefore$ $BA$ is a mean proportional between $AC$ and $AD$.

In like manner it can be shown that the triangles $ABC$, $DBC$ are similar; and that $BC$ is a mean proportional between $AC$ and $CD$.

Since $ABD$, $CBD$ are similar to $ABC$ they are similar to one another.

$$B\hat{A}D = D\hat{B}C$$

$$A\hat{B}D = B\hat{C}D$$

$$A\hat{D}B = B\hat{D}C,$$

$$\therefore\ DB : DC = BA : CB = AD : BD.$$

Hence $$DB : DC = AD : DB,$$

$$\therefore\ DC : DB = DB : DA.$$ [Prop. 19.

Hence $DB$ is a mean proportional between $DA$ and $DC$.

## Art. 117. EXAMPLE 41.

If in any triangle $ABC$, $BD$ is drawn to cut $AC$ at $D$ so that $B\hat{D}C$ is equal to $A\hat{B}C$, prove that the triangles $ABC$, $BCD$ are similar; that $BC$ is a mean proportional between $AC$ and $CD$, and that $AC : AB = BC : BD$.

# SECTION VI.

MISCELLANEOUS GEOMETRICAL PROPOSITIONS. Props. 33, 34.

### Art. 118. PROPOSITION XXXIII. (Euc. VI. 13.)

Enunciation. *To find a mean proportional between two given segments of straight lines.*

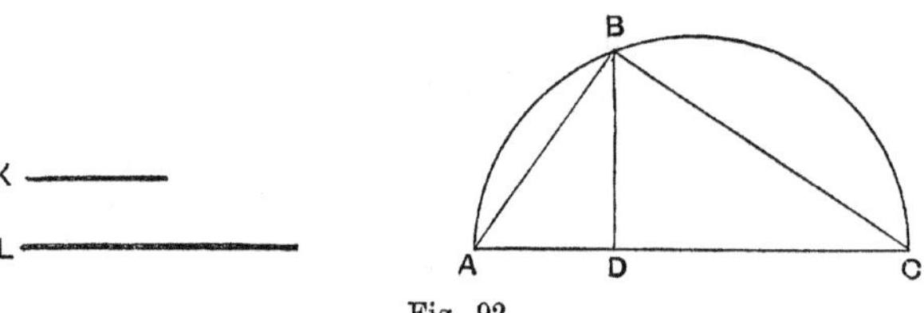


Fig. 92.

Let the given straight lines be $K$ and $L$.

Take a straight line $AD$ equal to $K$, and produce $AD$ to $C$, so that $DC$ is equal to $L$.

On $AC$ as diameter describe a semicircle.

Through $D$ draw $DB$ perpendicular to $AC$ to cut the semicircle at $B$.

Then $DB$ is the mean proportional between $K$ and $L$ required.

Join $AB$, $BC$.

Then $ABC$ being the angle in a semicircle is a right angle.

Also $BD$, being drawn perpendicular to $AC$ from the vertex $B$ of the right angle, is by Prop. 32 part (2) a mean proportional between $AD$ and $DC$.

$\therefore$ $BD$ is a mean proportional between $K$ and $L$.

### Art. 119. EXAMPLES.

**42.** Solve the problem of the last proposition by means of Proposition 32 (3) or (4).

**43.** If two circles touch each other and also touch a given straight line, prove that the part of the straight line between the points of contact is a mean proportional between the diameters of the circles.

**44.** If through the middle point $A$ of the arc $BAC$ of a circle, a chord be drawn cutting the chord of the arc $BC$ at $D$ and the circle again at $E$, prove that $AB$ is a mean proportional between $AD$ and $AE$.

**45.** If $C$ be the centre of a circle, $O$ a point outside it, $OT$ a tangent from $O$ to the circle, $TP$ a perpendicular from $T$ on $OC$, then prove that the radius of the circle is a mean proportional between $CO$ and $CP$.

## Art. 120. PROPOSITION XXXIV. (i). (Euc. VI. 3 and A, 1st Part.)

ENUNCIATION. *If the interior or exterior vertical angle of a triangle be bisected by a straight line which also cuts the base, the base is divided internally or externally in the ratio of the sides of the triangle.*

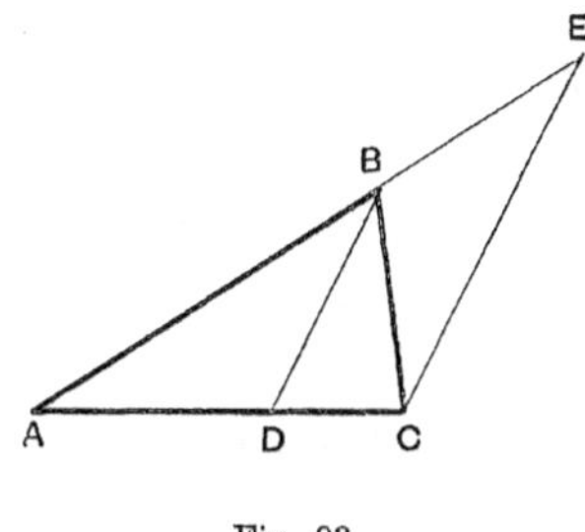


Fig. 93.

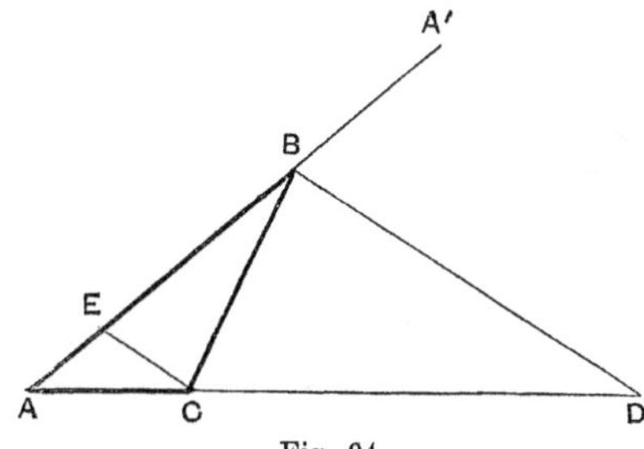


Fig. 94.

Let $ABC$ be a triangle.

Let $BD$ bisect the interior angle $ABC$ in Fig. 93, but the exterior angle $A'BC$ between $CB$ and $AB$ produced to $A'$ in Fig. 94.

Let $BD$ cut the base at $D$.

To prove that $AD : DC = AB : BC$.

Draw $CE$ parallel to $BD$ cutting $AB$ at $E$.

Then $B\hat{E}C = D\hat{B}A$ in Fig. 93 (or $D\hat{B}A'$ in Fig. 94)

$$= D\hat{B}C$$

$$= B\hat{C}E,$$

$$\therefore\ B\hat{E}C = B\hat{C}E,$$

$$\therefore\ BC = BE.$$

Since $ADC$, $ABE$ are cut by parallel lines $BD$, $CE$,

$$\therefore\ AD : DC = AB : BE, \qquad \text{[Prop. 13.}$$

$$\therefore\ AD : DC = AB : BC.$$

**Art. 121. PROPOSITION XXXIV.** (ii). **(Euc. VI. 3 and A, 2nd Part.)**

ENUNCIATION. *If the base of a triangle be divided internally or externally in the ratio of the sides of the triangle, the straight line drawn from the point of division to the vertex bisects the interior or exterior vertical angle.*

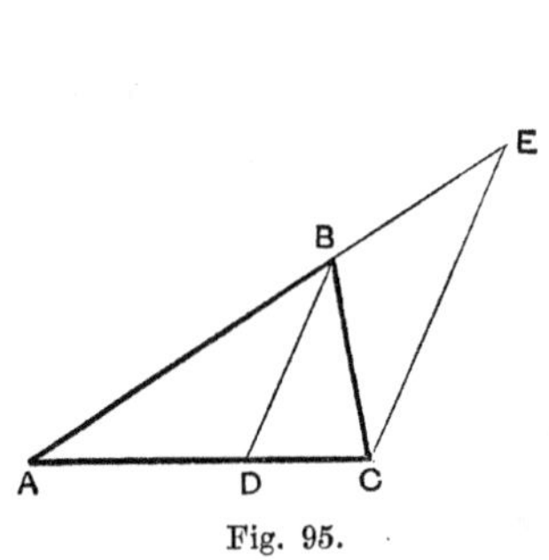


Fig. 95.

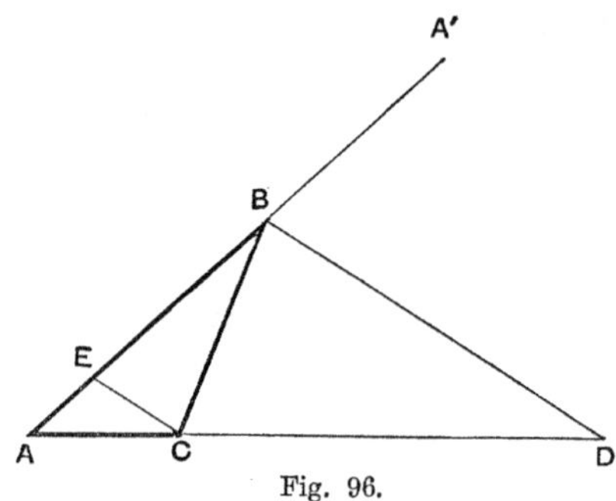


Fig. 96.

Let $ABC$ be a triangle.

Let $D$ divide the base $AC$, internally in Fig. 95, externally in Fig. 96, so that

$$AD : DC = AB : BC.$$

To prove that $DB$ bisects the interior angle $ABC$ in Fig. 95, but the exterior angle between $CB$ and $AB$ produced through $B$ in Fig. 96.

Join $DB$, and draw $CE$ parallel to $DB$ cutting $AB$ at $E$.

Then $$AD : DC = AB : BE,$$ [Prop. 13.

but $$AD : DC = AB : BC,$$

$$\therefore AB : BE = AB : BC,$$ [Prop. 10.

$$\therefore BE = BC,$$ [Prop. 21.

$$\therefore B\hat{C}E = B\hat{E}C.$$

Now $A\hat{B}D$ in Fig. 95, or $A'\hat{B}D$ in Fig. 96 $= B\hat{E}C$

$$= B\hat{C}E$$

$$= D\hat{B}C,$$

$\therefore A\hat{B}D$ in Fig. 95, or $A'\hat{B}D$ in Fig. 96 $= D\hat{B}C$.

Hence $DB$ bisects the interior vertical angle in Fig. 95, but the exterior vertical angle in Fig. 96.

## Art. 122. EXAMPLES.

46. If the internal and external angles at $B$ of the triangle $ABC$ be bisected by straight lines which cut the side $AC$ at $D$ and $E$ respectively, show that $A$, $D$, $C$, $E$ are four harmonic points.

47. By means of Proposition 34 construct the fourth harmonic to three given points $A$, $B$, $C$ on a straight line; considering separately the cases which arise according as the fourth harmonic is to be conjugate to $A$ or $B$ or $C$.

48. If $ABC$ be a triangle inscribed in a circle, $PQ$ a diameter of the circle perpendicular to $AC$, if $CB$ cut $PQ$ at $R$, and $AB$ cut $PQ$ at $S$, prove that

$$QR : RP = QS : SP.$$

Hence construct the fourth harmonic to three given points on a straight line.

49. Divide a given arc of a circle into two parts so that the chords of these parts may be to each other in a given ratio.

50. A point $P$ moves in a plane so that the ratio of its distances from two fixed points $A$, $B$ in that plane is always the same. Show that *in general* the locus of $P$ is a circle, the extremities of one diameter of which are the points dividing $AB$ internally and externally in the given ratio. What is the exceptional case?

51. The side $BC$ of a triangle $ABC$ is bisected at $D$, and the angles $ADB$, $ADC$ are bisected by the straight lines $DE$, $DF$ meeting $AC$, $AB$ at $E$, $F$ respectively. Prove that $EF$ is parallel to $BC$.

52. If the bisector of the angle $A$ of the triangle $ABC$ cut $BC$ at $D$, and if the bisector of the angle $B$ cut $AC$ at $E$, and if $DE$ be parallel to $AB$, prove that the triangle $ABC$ is isosceles.

53. If $ABC$ be a triangle, if $D$ be the middle point of $BC$, if any straight line through $D$ cut $AB$ at $E$, $AC$ at $F$, and a parallel through $A$ to $BC$ at $G$; then prove that $E$, $D$, $F$, $G$ are four harmonic points.

Hence show that if any point $O$ be joined to four harmonic points, they will be cut by any transversal in four harmonic points.

## Art. 123. *Def.* 20. HARMONIC LINES.

**If four straight lines be cut by any transversal in four harmonic points they are called four harmonic lines, or are said to form a harmonic pencil.**

# SECTION VII.

THE COMPOUNDING OF RATIOS. DUPLICATE RATIO. Props. 35—37.

**Art. 124.** The following proposition, No. 35, is necessary for, and proposition 56 below is also very useful in, the theory of the Compounding of Ratios.

### Art. 125. PROPOSITION XXXV*. (Euc. V. 22.)

ENUNCIATION 1.

If $A$, $B$, $C$ are three magnitudes of the same kind;
if $T$, $U$, $V$ are three magnitudes of the same kind;
if $A : B = T : U$,
and $B : C = U : V$,
prove that $A : C = T : V$.

ENUNCIATION 2.

*If $A$, $B$, $C$ are three magnitudes of the same kind;*
*if $T$, $U$, $V$ are three magnitudes of the same kind;*
*if* $[A, B] \simeq [T, U]$,
*and* $[B, C] \simeq [U, V]$,
*prove that* $[A, C] \simeq [T, V]$.

As in Prop. 22 it is convenient to use the second form of the conditions for the sameness of two scales in Prop. 8.

Take any integer $r$ in the first column, and any integer $s$ in the second column of the scales to be proved the same. It is necessary to show that

(1) If $rA < sC$, then $rT < sV$.
(2) If $rA > sC$, then $rT > sV$.
(3) If $rT < sV$, then $rA < sC$.
(4) If $rT > sV$, then $rA > sC$.

* See Note 9.

If $$rA < sC,$$
then since $rA$, $sC$, and $B$ are magnitudes of the same kind, by Prop. 7 integers $n$, $t$ exist such that
$$nrA < tB,$$
and $$tB < nsC.$$

Now $$\because\ nrA < tB,$$
the scale of $A$, $B$ shows the fact exhibited in Fig. 97.

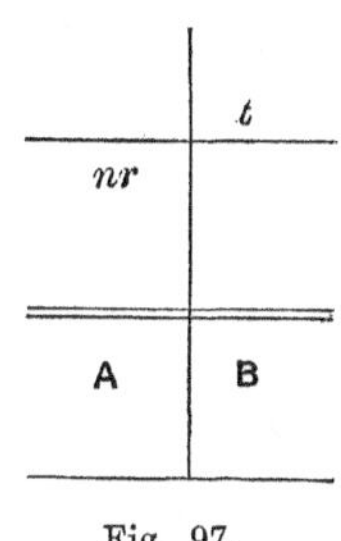

Fig. 97.

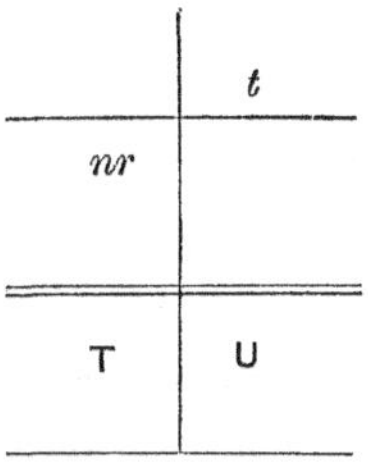

Fig. 98.

But $$[A, B] \simeq [T, U],$$
$\therefore$ the scale of $T$, $U$ shows the fact exhibited in Fig. 98,
$$\therefore\ nrT < tU \text{ .................................... (I).}$$

Again $$\because\ tB < nsC,$$
the scale of $B$, $C$ shows the fact exhibited in Fig. 99.

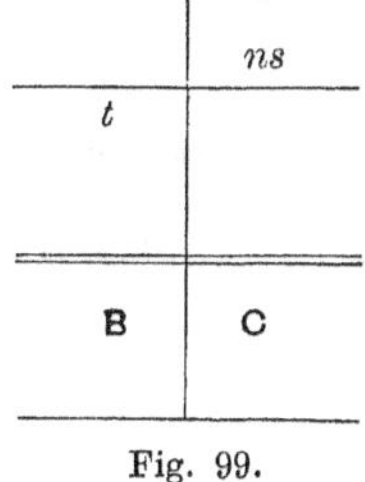

Fig. 99.

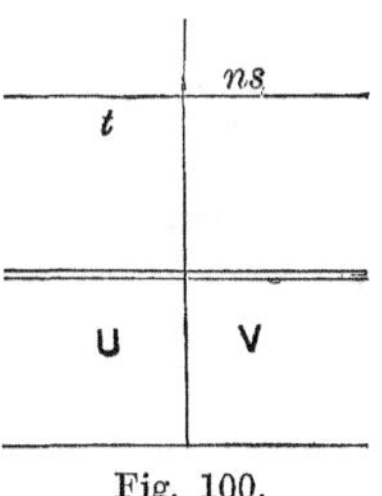

Fig. 100.

But $$[B, C] \simeq [U, V],$$
$\therefore$ the scale of $U$, $V$ shows the fact exhibited in Fig. 100,
$$\therefore\ tU < nsV \text{ .................................. (II).}$$

From (I) and (II) $$nrT < nsV,$$
$$\therefore\ rT < sV,$$
$$\therefore \text{ if } rA < sC, \text{ then } rT < sV \text{ ...................... (III).}$$

In like manner* if $rA > sC$, then $rT > sV$ ........................ (IV),

if $rT < sV$, then $rA < sC$ ............................(V),

if $rT > sV$, then $rA > sC$ ........................ (VI).

From (III), (IV), (V), (VI) it follows by Prop. 8 (ii) that

$$[A, C] \simeq [T, V].$$

## Art. 126. EXAMPLE 54.

Two circles whose centres are $C$ and $C'$ intercept equal chords $AB$ and $A'B'$ on a straight line cutting both circles.

The tangents at $A$ and $A'$ meet at $T$.

Prove that $$AT : A'T = AC : A'C'.$$

## Art. 127. THE COMPOUNDING OF RATIOS.

The development of this process is made in four stages.

STAGE 1. When it is necessary to determine the relative magnitude of two magnitudes, $A$ and $C$, of the same kind, it is often convenient not to make the comparison directly, but indirectly by taking another magnitude $B$ of the same kind as $A$ and $C$; and then comparing $A$ with $B$, and afterwards $B$ with $C$.

From this point of view the relative magnitude of $A$ and $C$ is considered to be determined by the relative magnitude of $A$ and $B$ and the relative magnitude of $B$ and $C$.

STAGE 2. Euclid expresses the general idea stated in the first stage† by saying that the ratio of $A$ to $C$ is compounded of the ratio of $A$ to $B$ and the ratio of $B$ to $C$.

* The proof of (IV) is obtained from that of (III) by reversing all the signs of inequality, and making the corresponding changes in the figures.

To obtain (V), since $rT < sV$, observe that integers $n$, $t$ exist by Prop. 7 such that

$$nrT < tU,$$

and $$tU < nsV,$$

and then proceed as in the proof of (III).

Or else it is obvious that the conditions given may be re-written

$$[T, U] \simeq [A, B],$$

and $$[U, V] \simeq [B, C].$$

Comparing these with the original form, it appears that they can be deduced from the original form by interchanging $A$ and $T$, $B$ and $U$, $C$ and $V$.

Hence it is permissible to make these changes in (III) and (IV), and the result is to give (V) and (VI).

† See the 23rd proposition of Euclid's Sixth Book, where the meaning is more easily understood than in the 5th definition of that book.

STAGE 3. *Def.* 21. THE PROCESS OF COMPOUNDING RATIOS.

**Let the ratios to be compounded be $P : Q$ and $T : U$.**

**Take any arbitrary magnitude $A$, and then find $B$ so that**

$$P : Q = A : B \qquad\text{(I)},$$

**and then find $C$ so that** $$T : U = B : C \qquad\text{(II)}.$$

**Then the ratio compounded of $P : Q$ and $T : U$ is the ratio compounded of $A : B$ and $B : C$, and is therefore $A : C$ by the statement in the second stage.**

This process* contains an arbitrary element, viz. $A$.

STAGE 4. In order to justify the process described in the preceding stage, it is necessary to show that the presence of the arbitrary element in the third stage has no influence on the value of the resulting ratio.

Suppose that instead of $A$, the magnitude $A'$ had been selected, and that $B'$ and $C'$ had then been found so that

$$P : Q = A' : B' \qquad\text{(III)},$$

$$T : U = B' : C' \qquad\text{(IV)}.$$

Then the resulting ratio would be that compounded of $A' : B'$ and $B' : C'$, and would therefore be $A' : C'$.

In order that this may agree with the previous result, it is necessary to show that

$$A : C = A' : C' \qquad\text{(V)}.$$

From (I) and (III) by Prop. 10

$$A : B = A' : B' \qquad\text{(VI)}.$$

From (II) and (IV) by Prop. 10

$$B : C = B' : C' \qquad\text{(VII)}.$$

From (VI) and (VII) by Prop. 35, the proportion (V) follows.

Hence the process in the third stage always leads to the same value of the resulting ratio, whatever be the value of the arbitrary element.

This is the justification of the process described in the third stage.

* It should be noted that this process assumes the existence of $B$ and $C$, when $A$ has been chosen arbitrarily, the proof of which depends on the Fundamental Proposition in the Theory of Scales.

## Art. 128. ARITHMETICAL APPLICATION OF THE PROCESS FOR COMPOUNDING RATIOS.

To compound the ratio $r : s$ with the ratio $u : v$ where $r$, $s$, $u$, $v$ are positive integers.

$$\left.\begin{array}{l} r : s = ru : su \\ u : v = su : sv \end{array}\right\} \text{by Prop. 9.}$$

Hence $\quad r : s$ compounded with $u : v$

$= ru : su$ compounded with $su : sv$

$= ru : sv$

by the definition of the ratio compounded of other ratios in Art. 127, Stage 2.

Now the measure of $r : s$ is $\frac{r}{s}$;

the measure of $u : v$ is $\frac{u}{v}$; [Arts. 44, 64

and the measure of $ru : sv$ is $\frac{ru}{sv}$.

Observe further that $\frac{ru}{sv}$ is defined to be the Arithmetical Product of $\frac{r}{s}$ and $\frac{u}{v}$, the result being written

$$\frac{r}{s} \times \frac{u}{v} = \frac{ru}{sv}.$$

Hence this arithmetical theorem corresponds to the theorem that

$r : s$ compounded with $u : v = ru : sv$.

## Art. 129. *Def.* 22. DUPLICATE RATIO.

**If a ratio be compounded with itself the resulting ratio is called the duplicate ratio of the original ratio.**

Thus if $A : B$ be compounded with $A : B$, the resulting ratio is called the duplicate ratio of $A : B$.

## Art. 130. PROPOSITION XXXVI.

ENUNCIATION. *If three magnitudes be in proportion the first has to the third the duplicate ratio of the first to the second.*

Let $A : B = B : C$.

Then if $A : B$ be compounded with $A : B$, the result is the same as if $A : B$ be compounded with $B : C$, and is therefore $A : C$. [Art. 127, Stage 2.

Hence $A : C$ is the duplicate ratio of $A : B$, if $A : B = B : C$.

## Art. 131. PROPOSITION XXXVII.

ENUNCIATION. *If two ratios be equal, their duplicate ratios are also equal.*

If $A : B = C : D$ ....................................(1),

it is required to prove that the duplicate ratio of $A : B$ is equal to that of $C : D$.

Take $E$ so that $A : B = B : E$....................................(2),

and $F$ so that $C : D = D : F$....................................(3).

Then by (1), (2), (3) and Prop. 10

$B : E = D : F$....................................(4).

Hence from (1) and (4) $A : E = C : F$, [Prop. 35.

But by (2) $A : E$ is the duplicate ratio of $A : B$ [Prop. 36.

and by (3) $C : F$ is the duplicate ratio of $C : D$ [Prop. 36.

$\therefore$ the duplicate ratio of $A : B$ is equal to the duplicate ratio of $C : D$.

# SECTION VIII.

AREAS. Props. 38—49.

### Art. 132. PROPOSITION XXXVIII (i). (Euc. VI. 16, 1st Part.)

ENUNCIATION. *If four straight lines are proportional, the rectangle contained by the extremes is equal to the rectangle contained by the means.*

Let $K$, $L$, $M$, $P$ be the straight lines, such that

$$K : L = M : P,$$

it is required to prove that the rectangle contained by $K$ and $P$ is equal to that contained by $L$ and $M$.

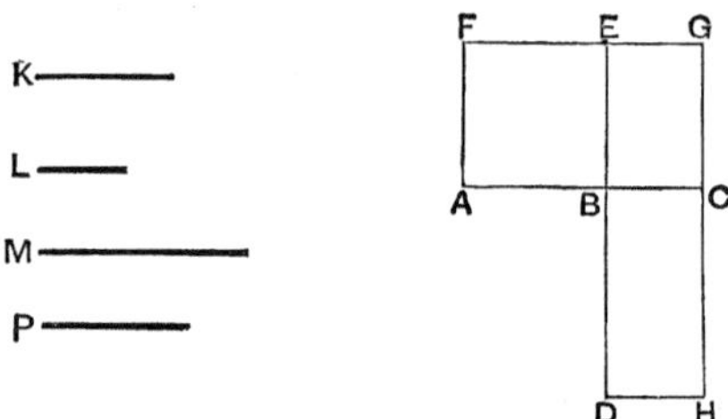


Fig. 101.

Take $AB$ equal to $K$.

Produce $AB$ to $C$ so that $BC$ is equal to $L$.

Through $B$ draw $BD$ equal to $M$ perpendicular to $AB$, and produce $DB$ to $E$ so that $BE$ is equal to $P$.

Complete the rectangles $ABEF$, $BCGE$, $BCHD$.

Since rectangles having equal altitudes are proportional to their bases (Prop. 17)

$$ABEF : BCGE = AB : BC = K : L,$$

$$BCHD : BCGE = BD : BE = M : P.$$

Now $K : L = M : P$,

$$\therefore ABEF : BCGE = BCHD : BCGE,$$

$$\therefore ABEF = BCHD. \qquad \text{[Prop. 21.}$$

Now $ABEF$ is the rectangle contained by $AB$ and $BE$, i.e. by $K$ and $P$. Whilst $BCHD$ is the rectangle contained by $BC$ and $BD$, i.e. by $L$ and $M$.

$\therefore$ the rectangle contained by $K$ and $P$ is equal to that contained by $L$ and $M$.

### Art. 133. PROPOSITION XXXVIII (ii). (Euc. VI. 16, 2nd Part.)

ENUNCIATION. *Let there be four straight lines, which taken in a definite order are K, L, M, P; and let it be given that the rectangle contained by the first and fourth, K and P, is equal to the rectangle contained by the second and third, L and M; to prove that*

$$K : L = M : P.$$

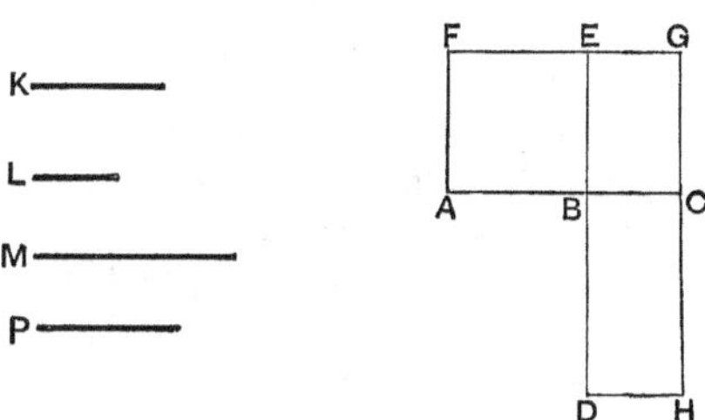


Fig. 102.

Make the same construction as in the preceding part of the proposition.

The rectangle contained by $K$ and $P$ is the rectangle contained by $AB$ and $BE$ and is therefore $ABEF$.

The rectangle contained by $L$ and $M$ is the rectangle contained by $BC$ and $BD$, and is therefore $BCHD$.

$\therefore ABEF$ is given equal to $BCHD$.

$$\therefore ABEF : BCGE = BCHD : BCGE, \qquad \text{[Prop. 20.}$$

but $ABEF : BCGE = AB : BC = K : L$, [Prop. 17.

and $BCHD : BCGE = BD : BE = M : P$, [Prop. 17.

$$\therefore K : L = M : P. \qquad \text{[Prop. 10.}$$

## Art. 134. COROLLARY TO PROPOSITION 38. (Euc. VI. 17.)

PART 1. *If three straight lines are proportionals, the rectangle contained by the extremes is equal to the square on the mean.*

PART 2. *Let there be three straight lines, which taken in a definite order are K, L, and P; and let it be given that the rectangle contained by the first and third, K and P, is equal to the square on the second, L, then it will follow that*

$$K : L = L : P.$$

The first part is the particular case of Proposition 38 (i), and the second part the particular case of Proposition 38 (ii), when $M = L$.

## Art. 135. EXAMPLES.

**55.** Let $C$ be the centre of a circle, $O$ any point in its plane; let $A$ and $B$ be the extremities of the diameter through $O$; let $P$ and $Q$ be the extremities of any chord through $O$. Prove that the circle drawn through $C$, $P$ and $Q$ cuts $OC$ in a point $D$ which is the same for all directions of the chord $OPQ$, and show that

$$OA : OD = OC : OB.$$

**56.** (i) Let $A$ be the centre of a circle, $B$ a point outside it, $BD$ and $BE$ tangents to the circle, $C$ the point in which $DE$ cuts $AB$, $BFG$ a straight line through $B$ cutting the circle at $F$ and $G$; then prove that the rectangle $BA \cdot BC$ is equal to the rectangle $BF \cdot BG$. Prove that $CD$ bisects the angle $FCG$, and that if $CD$ cut $FG$ at $H$, then $B$, $F$, $H$, $G$ are four harmonic points.

(ii) Let $A$ be the centre of a circle, $B$ a point inside the circle, and let any chord $GBF$ be drawn through $B$, and produced to $H$ so that $G$, $B$, $F$, $H$ are four harmonic points, prove that the locus of $H$ is a straight line which cuts $AB$ at right angles at a point $C$ such that the rectangle $BA \cdot BC$ is equal to the rectangle $BF \cdot BG$.

**57.** If $A$, $B$, $C$, $D$ are four harmonic points and $O$ the middle point between the two conjugate points $A$ and $C$, prove that the rectangle contained by $OB$ and $OD$ is equal to the square on $OC$.

## Art. 136. *Def.* 23. POLE AND POLAR.

**If through any point $O$ a straight line be drawn cutting a circle at $P$ and $Q$, and on $OPQ$ a point $R$ be taken so that $O$, $P$, $R$, $Q$ are four harmonic points, $O$ and $R$ being conjugates; then the locus of $R$ is called the polar line of $O$, and $O$ is called the pole of the locus of $R$.**

It is a result of Example 56 that the polar line is a straight line.

## Art. 137. EXAMPLES.

**58.** If $C$ be the centre of a circle, $O$ any point in its plane and $T$ the foot of the perpendicular from $C$ on to the polar line of $O$, then prove that the rectangle contained by $CO$ and $CT$ is equal to the square on the radius of the circle.

**59.** If $A$ lie on the polar of $B$ with regard to a circle, show that $B$ lies on the polar of $A$ with regard to that circle.

(Two such points as $A$, $B$ are said to be conjugate with regard to the circle.)

**60.** If two circles cut at right angles prove that the extremities of any diameter of either circle are conjugate points with regard to the other circle.

**61.** If $A$, $B$ be two points, and if from $A$ a perpendicular $AP$ be drawn to the polar line of $B$ with regard to a circle whose centre is $C$, and if from $B$ a perpendicular $BQ$ be drawn to the polar line of $A$, prove that

$$CA : CB = AP : BQ,$$

and show that the triangles $CAP$, $CBQ$ are similar.

**62.** Let $C$ be the centre of a circle, $V$ any fixed point in its plane, let $CV$ cut the circumference at $A$, and let a point $P$ be taken on $CV$ so that the rectangle $CV.CP$ is equal to the square on $CA$. Let a straight line $PY$ be drawn through $P$ perpendicular to $CP$, and let $PY$ be cut by any straight line through $V$ in $W$, and by a perpendicular through $C$ to $VW$ in $X$, prove that the rectangle $PX.PW$ will always be equal to the rectangle $CP.PV$ in whatever direction the straight line $VW$ may be drawn.

## Art. 138. *Def.* 24. INVERSE LOCUS. CENTRE OF INVERSION.

**If from any point $O$ a straight line be drawn to cut any curve at $P$, and on $OP$ a point $Q$ be taken so that the rectangle $OP.OQ$ has a constant area, then the locus of $Q$ is called the inverse of the locus of $P$ with regard to $O$ as centre (or origin) of inversion.**

The side of the square whose area is equal to the constant rectangle $OP.OQ$ is called the radius of inversion.

Also $P$ and $Q$ are said to be inverse points with regard to the circle whose centre is $O$, and whose radius is the radius of inversion.

## Art. 139. EXAMPLES.

**63.** If the locus of $P$ is a circle, show that the inverse locus is generally a circle, but will be a straight line if the centre of inversion be a point on the circle on which $P$ lies.

**64.** If the locus of $P$ is a straight line show that the inverse locus is a circle passing through the centre of inversion.

**65.** If two circles or a straight line and a circle or two straight lines intersect one another, show that their angle of intersection is equal to the angle of intersection of their inverse loci.

### Art. 140. *Def.* 25. THE RADICAL AXIS OF TWO CIRCLES.

**The locus of points from which tangents drawn to two circles are of equal length is called the radical axis of the two circles.**

### Art. 141. EXAMPLES.

**66.** If two circles intersect, show that the straight line joining their points of intersection is their radical axis.

If they do not intersect, show that the radical axis is perpendicular to the line joining the centres of the circles, and cuts it at a point which is such that double the distance of this point from the point half way between the centres of the circles is a fourth proportional to the distance between the centres of the circles, the sum of their radii and the difference of their radii.

**67.** Show that the difference between the squares of the tangents from any point $P$ to two circles is equal to twice the rectangle contained by the perpendicular from $P$ on the radical axis, and the distance between the centres of the circles.

**68.** Show how to choose the centre and the radius of inversion so that two given circles may be inverted each into itself.

### Art. 142. PROPOSITION XXXIX.

ENUNCIATION. *The rectangle contained by the diagonals of a quadrilateral cannot be greater than the sum of the rectangles contained by opposite sides.* (It may be equal, and in that case a circle can be described through the vertices of the quadrilateral.)

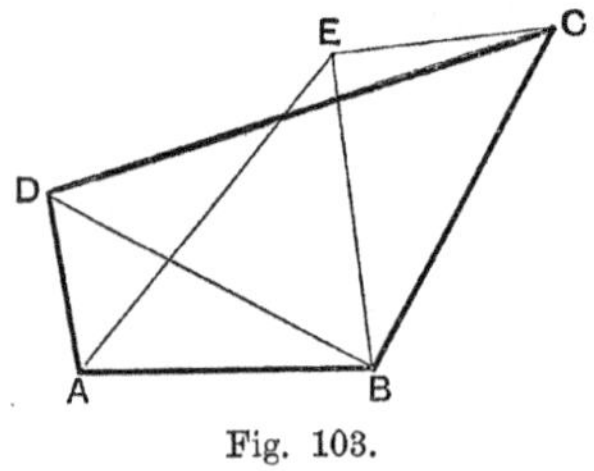


Fig. 103.

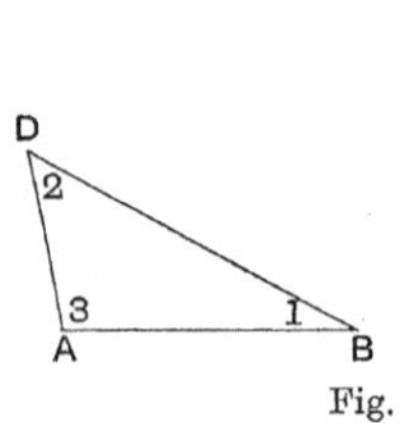


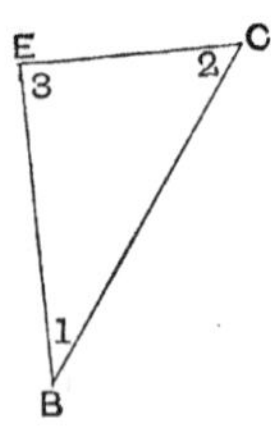


Fig. 104.

Let $ABCD$ be a quadrilateral.

It is required to prove that the rectangle $AC.BD$ cannot be greater than the sum of the rectangles $AD.BC$ and $AB.CD$.

On $BC$ describe the triangle $BCE$ similar to $ABD$, so that the side $BC$ of $BCE$ may correspond to the side $BD$ of $ABD$.

Then
$$C\hat{B}E = A\hat{B}D$$
$$B\hat{C}E = B\hat{D}A$$
$$B\hat{E}C = B\hat{A}D.$$

Also
$$BD : BC = DA : CE = AB : EB.$$

From the first and second ratios it follows by Prop. 38 (i) that
$$\text{rect. } BD.CE = \text{rect. } AD.BC.$$

Also from the first and third ratios
$$BD : BC = BA : BE,$$
but also
$$D\hat{B}C = D\hat{B}E + E\hat{B}C$$
$$= D\hat{B}E + D\hat{B}A$$
$$= A\hat{B}E.$$

Hence by Prop. 28 the triangles $DBC$, $ABE$ are similar.

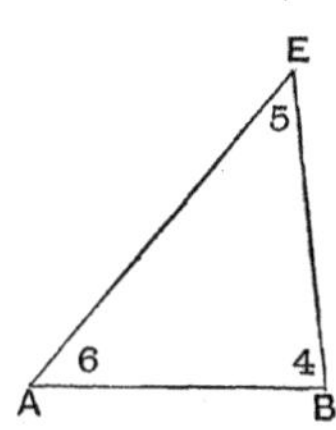

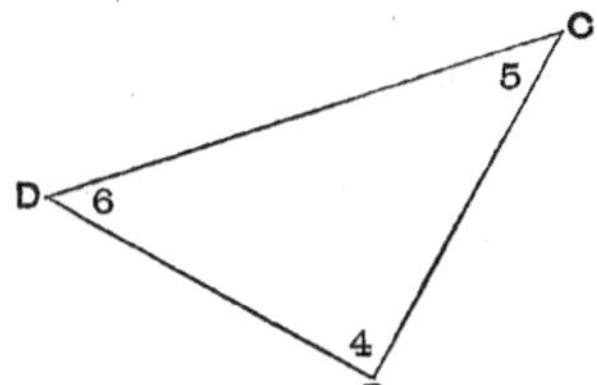


Fig. 105.

The side $BD$ corresponds to $BA$,
the side $BC$ corresponds to $BE$,
and the side $CD$ corresponds to $AE$.
$$\therefore\ BD : BA = DC : AE = CB : EB.$$

From the first and second ratios by Prop. 38 (i)
$$\text{rect. } BD.AE = \text{rect. } AB.CD.$$

Now it has been shown that
$$\text{rect. } BD.CE = \text{rect. } AD.BC,$$
$$\therefore\ \text{rect. } BD.AE + \text{rect. } BD.CE = \text{rect. } AB.CD + \text{rect. } AD.BC.$$

Now $AC$ cannot be greater than $AE + EC$.

(The case in which $AC$ is equal to $AE + EC$ will be considered below.)

$\therefore$ rect. $BD.AC$ cannot be greater than rect. $BD.AE$ + rect. $BD.CE$.

$\therefore$ rect. $BD.AC$ cannot be greater than rect. $AB.CD$ + rect. $AD.BC$.

If $$AC = AE + EC,$$

then $E$ lies on $AC$,

and rect. $BD.AC$ = rect. $AB.CD$ + rect. $AD.BC$.

Now $$B\hat{C}E = B\hat{D}A,$$

whilst in this case $$B\hat{C}E = B\hat{C}A.$$

$$\therefore \; B\hat{C}A = B\hat{D}A,$$

and therefore the circle circumscribing $ABD$ passes through $C$.

Hence a circle can be described about the vertices of the quadrilateral $ABCD$.

**Art. 143.** It is interesting to examine what happens when $D$ and $C$ are points on the straight line $AB$.

In this case the straight line can be regarded as a circle of infinite radius.

Hence taking the points on the line in the order $A$, $B$, $C$, $D$ the lines corresponding to the diagonals are $AC$, $BD$; whilst $AB$, $CD$ correspond to one pair of opposite sides; and $BC$, $AD$ to the other pair.

Hence rect. $AC.BD$ = rect. $AB.CD$ + rect. $BC.AD$.

This result is easily verified.

## Art. 144. PROPOSITION XL. (Euc. VI. 23.)

ENUNCIATION. *The areas of equiangular parallelograms are to one another in the ratio which is compounded of the ratios of their sides.*

Since the parallelograms are equiangular it is always possible to place one on the other, so that a vertex of the one coincides with a vertex of the other, and the sides of the one parallelogram which pass through that vertex fall upon the sides of the other which pass through that vertex.

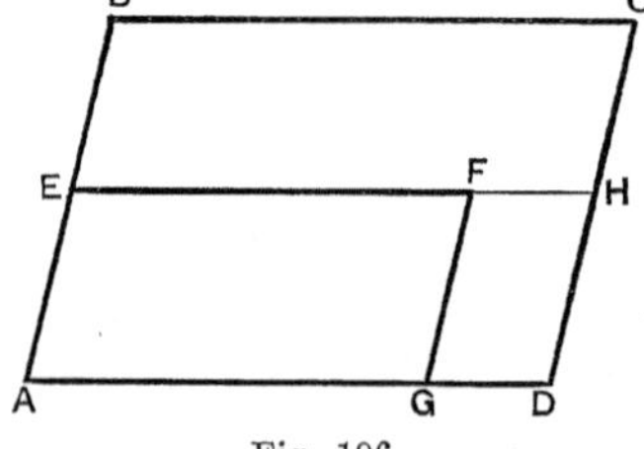

Fig. 106.

When this has been done let the parallelograms be $ABCD$, $AEFG$.

Since $$A\hat{B}C = A\hat{E}F,$$

$EF$ is parallel to $BC$.

Produce $EF$ to cut $CD$ at $H$.

Now parallelogram $ABCD$ : parallelogram $AEFG$

is equal to the ratio compounded of

parallelogram $ABCD$ : parallelogram $AEHD$

and parallelogram $AEHD$ : parallelogram $AEFG$, [Art. 127.

and is therefore equal to the ratio compounded of

$AB : AE$ and $AD : AG$. [Prop. 17.

**Art. 145.** A slight addition to the construction will give the value of the ratio compounded of $AB : AE$ and $AD : AG$ as the ratio of two lines.

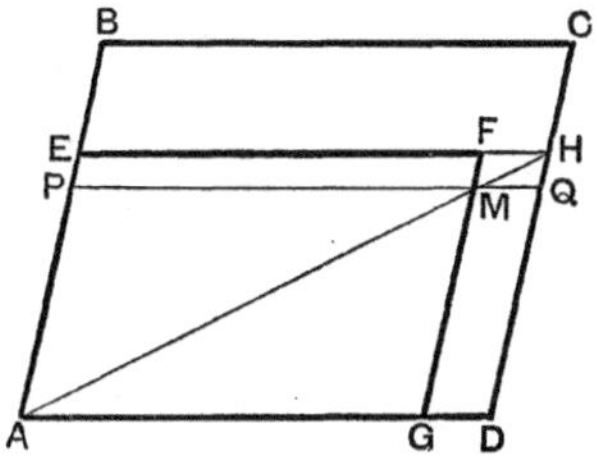

Produce $EF$ to cut $CD$ in $H$.

Join $AH$, and let it cut $FG$ in $M$.

Through $M$ draw $PMQ$ parallel to $AD$, cutting $AB$ at $P$ and $CD$ at $Q$.

Then the parallelograms $AEFG$ and $APQD$ are equal in area.

Fig. 107.

$\therefore\ ABCD : AEFG = ABCD : ABQD$

$= AB : AP$. [Prop. 17.

To see that $AB : AP$ is the ratio compounded of $AB : AE$ and $AD : AG$, observe that $AB : AP$ is the ratio compounded of $AB : AE$ and $AE : AP$.

But $AE : AP = AH : AM$ [Prop. 13.

$= AD : AG$. [Prop. 13.

$\therefore\ AB : AP =$ ratio compounded of $AB : AE$ and $AD : AG$.

## Art. 146. NOTE.

If the ratios $AB : AE$ and $AD : AG$ be given, the construction of the figure determines a point $P$ such that the ratio $AB : AP$ is the ratio compounded of $AB : AE$ and $AD : AG$.

## Art. 147. COROLLARIES.

(1) *Two rectangles have to one another the ratio compounded of the ratios of their sides.*

From (1) and the definition of duplicate ratio (Art. 129) it follows that

(2) *Two squares are to one another in the duplicate ratio of their sides.*

### Art. 148. EXAMPLE 69.

The triangles $ABC$, $DEF$ have the angles at $A$ and $D$ either equal or supplementary; prove that the triangles are to one another in the ratio compounded of $AB : DE$ and $AC : DF$.

### Art. 149. PROPOSITION XLI.

ENUNCIATION. *The ratio of the areas of two triangles is the ratio compounded of the ratio of their bases and the ratio of their altitudes.*

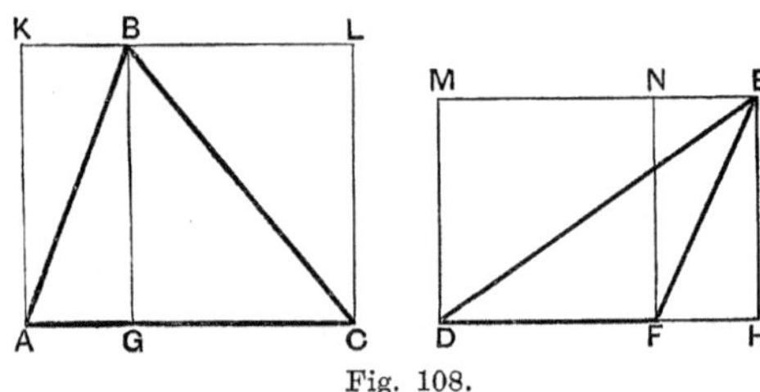


Fig. 108.

Let $ABC$, $DEF$ be two triangles, standing on the bases $AC$, $DF$ respectively.

Draw $BG$ perpendicular to $AC$, $EH$ perpendicular to $DF$.

Then $AC : DF$ is the ratio of the bases of the triangles, and $BG : EH$ is the ratio of their altitudes.

It is required to show that

$$\triangle ABC : \triangle DEF = \text{ratio compounded of } AC : DF \text{ and } BG : EH.$$

Draw the rectangle $AKLC$ on the base $AC$ having the same altitude as the triangle $ABC$.

Draw the rectangle $DMNF$ on the base $DF$ having the same altitude as the triangle $DEF$.

Then $\text{rect. } AKLC = 2\triangle ABC,$

and $\text{rect. } DMNF = 2\triangle DEF.$

$\therefore \triangle ABC : \triangle DEF = \text{rect. } AKLC : \text{rect. } DMNF$ [Art. 42.

$= \text{ratio compounded of } AC : DF \text{ and } AK : DM$

$= \text{ratio compounded of } AC : DF \text{ and } BG : EH.$

### Art. 150. EXAMPLE 70.

If $ABC$ be a triangle, and if $BE$, $CF$ be drawn perpendicular to the sides $AC$, $AB$ respectively; prove that the triangle $ABE$ is to the triangle $ACF$ as the square on $AB$ is to the square on $AC$.

## Art. 151. PROPOSITION XLII. (Euc. VI. 19.)

ENUNCIATION. *The areas of similar triangles are to one another in the duplicate ratio of corresponding sides.**

Let the triangles $ABC$, $DEF$ be similar.

Let the side $AC$ correspond to the side $DF$.

To prove that $\triangle ABC : \triangle DEF$

$= \text{duplicate ratio of } AC : DF.$

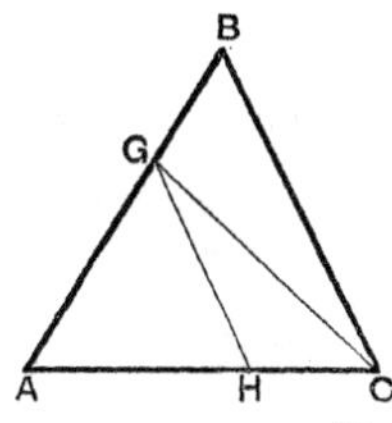


Fig. 109.

Take $AG$ on $AB$ equal to $DE$, the side corresponding to $AB$;

and $AH$ on $AC$ equal to $DF$, the side corresponding to $AC$.

Join $GH$.

Then the triangles $AGH$, $DEF$ have

$$AG = DE,$$
$$AH = DF,$$
$$G\hat{A}H = E\hat{D}F.$$

∴ they are congruent.

$$\therefore \; A\hat{H}G = D\hat{F}E = A\hat{C}B.$$

∴ $GH$ is parallel to $BC$.

Now join $GC$.

Now $\triangle ABC : \triangle DEF = \triangle ABC : \triangle AGH$

$= \text{ratio compounded of } \triangle ABC : \triangle AGC \text{ and } \triangle AGC : \triangle AGH.$

But $\triangle ABC : \triangle AGC = AB : AG$ [Prop. 17.

$= AB : DE$

$= AC : DF$

ince the triangles $ABC$, $DEF$ are similar.

* The proof here given is of the same kind as that in Prop. 40.

Also $\triangle AGC : \triangle AGH = AC : AH$ [Prop. 17.

$= AC : DF.$

$\therefore$ $\triangle ABC : \triangle DEF =$ ratio compounded of $AC : DF$ and $AC : DF$

$=$ duplicate ratio of $AC : DF.$

### Art. 152. COROLLARY.

From Prop. 42 and the second Corollary in Art. 147 it follows that

*The areas of similar triangles are proportional to the squares on corresponding sides*.*

This result may also be stated thus:

*The areas of similar triangles are proportional to the squares of their linear dimensions.*

### Art. 153. PROPOSITION XLIII. (Euc. V. 12.)

ENUNCIATION 1. If there be any number of equal ratios in which the magnitudes are all of the same kind, then the ratio of any antecedent to its consequent is equal to the ratio of the sum of the antecedents to the sum of the consequents; i.e. if

$$A : B = C : D = E : F,$$

then $$A : B = A + C + E : B + D + F.$$

ENUNCIATION 2. *If there be any number of pairs of magnitudes all of the same kind, and if each pair have the same scale; then this scale is also the scale of the two magnitudes, of which the first is the sum of the first terms of the pairs and the second is the sum of the second terms of the pairs; i.e. if*

$$[A, B] \simeq [C, D] \simeq [E, F],$$

*then* $$[A, B] \simeq [A + C + E,\ B + D + F].$$

Take any two integers, $r$ in the first column, and $s$ in the second column of the scale of $A$, $B$.

* See Note 10.

Then there are the three alternatives

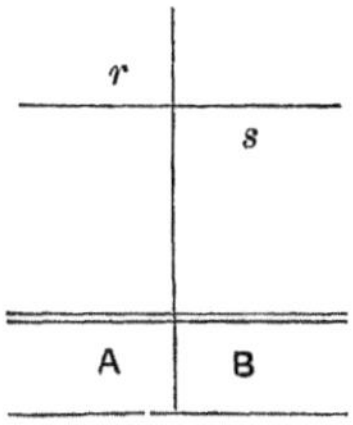

Fig. 110.

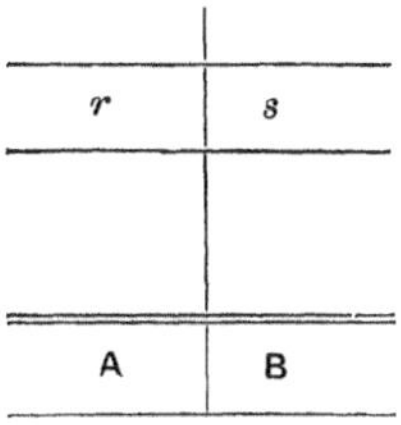

Fig. 111.

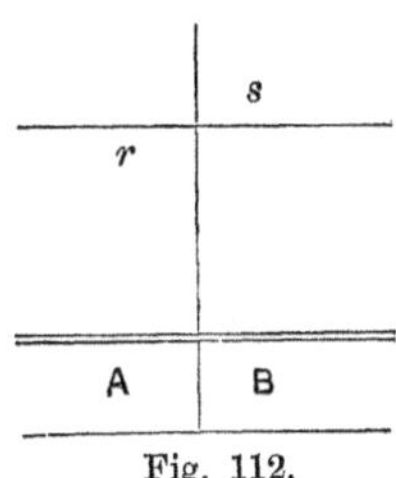


Fig. 112.

which represent

$rA > sB$ $\qquad$ $rA = sB$ $\qquad$ $rA < sB$.

Since $[A, B] \simeq [C, D] \simeq [E, F]$
there are the figures

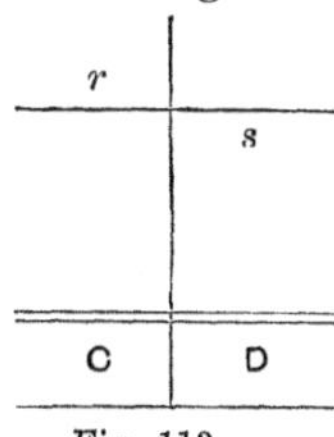


Fig. 113.

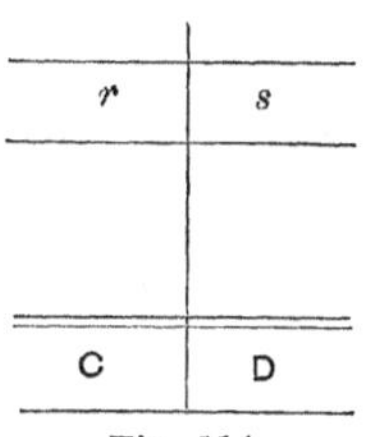


Fig. 114.

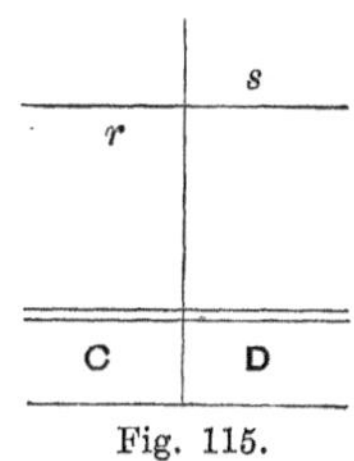


Fig. 115.

which represent

$rC > sD$ $\qquad$ $rC = sD$ $\qquad$ $rC < sD$

and the figures

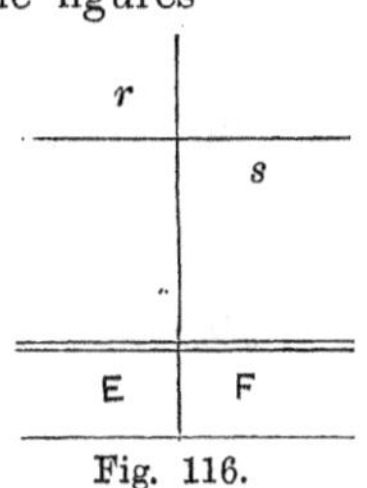


Fig. 116.

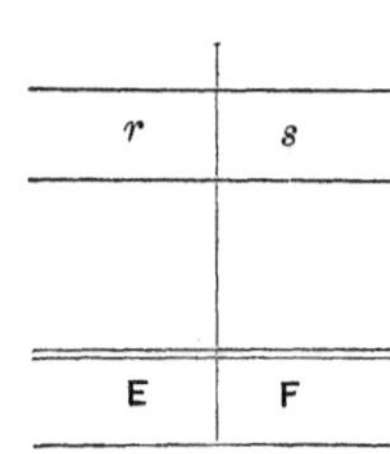


Fig. 117.

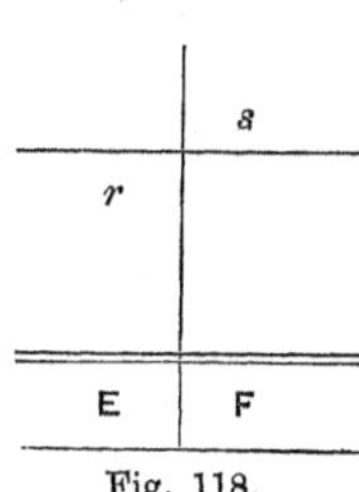


Fig. 118.

which represent

$rE > sF$ $\qquad$ $rE = sF$ $\qquad$ $rE < sF$.

Hence, when

$rA > sB$ $\qquad$ $rA = sB$ $\qquad$ $rA < sB$

it is also true that

$rC > sD$ $\qquad$ $rC = sD$ $\qquad$ $rC < sD$

$rE > sF$ $\qquad$ $rE = sF$ $\qquad$ $rE < sF$

and therefore also

$r(A+C+E)>s(B+D+F)$; $r(A+C+E)=s(B+D+F)$; $r(A+C+E)<s(B+D+F)$

which are represented by the figures

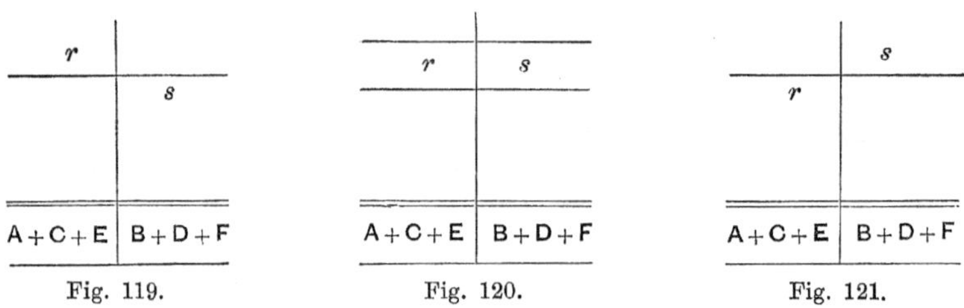


Fig. 119. Fig. 120. Fig. 121.

Comparing figures 119, 120, 121 with figures 110, 111, 112 respectively, it follows that

$$[A, B] \simeq [A + C + E,\ B + D + F].$$

## Art. 154. EXAMPLE 71.

The perimeters of similar triangles (or similar rectilineal figures) are to one another in the ratio of corresponding sides.

## Art. 155. PROPOSITION XLIV. (Euc. VI. 20.)

ENUNCIATION. *The areas of similar rectilineal figures are to one another in the duplicate ratio of corresponding sides.*

Let $A_1B_1C_1D_1$ and $A_2B_2C_2D_2$ be similar figures, and $A_1B_1$, $A_2B_2$ corresponding sides.

To prove that

$$A_1B_1C_1D_1 : A_2B_2C_2D_2 = \text{duplicate ratio of } A_1B_1 : A_2B_2.$$

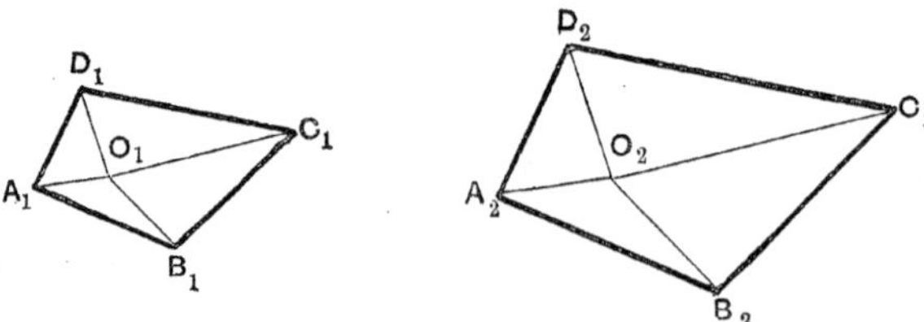


Fig. 122.

Taking the figure of Proposition 31 it was proved that the triangles $O_1A_1B_1$, $O_2A_2B_2$ were similar, as were also $O_1B_1C_1$ and $O_2B_2C_2$, $O_1C_1D_1$ and $O_2C_2D_2$, $O_1D_1A_1$ and $O_2D_2A_2$.

Hence by Prop. 42

$$\triangle O_1A_1B_1 : \triangle O_2A_2B_2 = \text{duplicate ratio of } A_1B_1 : A_2B_2,$$
$$\triangle O_1B_1C_1 : \triangle O_2B_2C_2 = \text{duplicate ratio of } B_1C_1 : B_2C_2,$$
$$\triangle O_1C_1D_1 : \triangle O_2C_2D_2 = \text{duplicate ratio of } C_1D_1 : C_2D_2,$$
$$\triangle O_1D_1A_1 : \triangle O_2D_2A_2 = \text{duplicate ratio of } D_1A_1 : D_2A_2.$$

But since the figures are similar

$$A_1B_1 : A_2B_2 = B_1C_1 : B_2C_2 = C_1D_1 : C_2D_2 = D_1A_1 : D_2A_2.$$

Hence by Prop. 37 the duplicate ratios of these ratios are equal.

$$\therefore \triangle O_1A_1B_1 : \triangle O_2A_2B_2 = \triangle O_1B_1C_1 : \triangle O_2B_2C_2 = \triangle O_1C_1D_1 : \triangle O_2C_2D_2 = \triangle O_1D_1A_1 : \triangle O_2D_2A_2.$$

Hence by Prop. 43

$$\triangle O_1A_1B_1 : \triangle O_2A_2B_2$$
$$= \triangle O_1A_1B_1 + \triangle O_1B_1C_1 + \triangle O_1C_1D_1 + \triangle O_1D_1A_1 : \triangle O_2A_2B_2 + \triangle O_2B_2C_2 + \triangle O_2C_2D_2 + \triangle O_2D_2A_2$$
$$= \text{figure } A_1B_1C_1D_1 : \text{figure } A_2B_2C_2D_2.$$

$$\therefore \text{ figure } A_1B_1C_1D_1 : \text{figure } A_2B_2C_2D_2 = \text{duplicate ratio of } A_1B_1 : A_2B_2.$$

### Art. 156. COROLLARY.

From this and Art. 147 (2) it follows that *the areas of similar rectilineal figures are proportional to the squares described on corresponding sides.*

### Art. 157. PROPOSITION XLV. (i). (Euc. VI. 22, 1st Part.)

ENUNCIATION. *Let there be four straight lines $A$, $B$, $C$, $D$ which are in proportion.*

*Let two similar rectilinear figures be similarly described on $A$ and $B$.*

*Let two similar rectilinear figures be similarly described on $C$ and $D$.*

*It is required to prove that*

*the figure on $A$ : the figure on $B$*
*= the figure on $C$ : the figure on $D$.*

Let the similar figures similarly described on $A$ and $B$ be called $U$ and $V$ respectively.

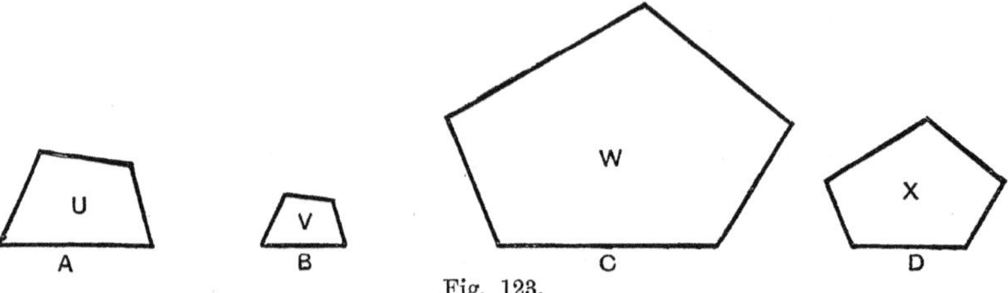


Fig. 123.

Then $U : V =$ duplicate ratio of $A : B$. [Prop. 44.

Let the similar figures similarly described on $C$ and $D$ be called $W$ and $X$ respectively.

Then $W : X =$ duplicate ratio of $C : D$. [Prop. 44.

Now $A : B = C : D$,

$\therefore$ the duplicate ratio of $A : B$

$=$ the duplicate ratio of $C : D$, [Prop. 37.

$\therefore$ $U : V = W : X$.

### Art. 158. PROPOSITION XLV. (ii). (Euc. VI. 22, 2nd Part.)

ENUNCIATION. *Let there be four straight lines $A$, $B$, $C$, $D$.*

*Let two similar figures be similarly described on $A$ and $B$.*

*Let two similar figures be similarly described on $C$ and $D$.*

*Let it be given that*

*the figure on $A$ : the figure on $B$*

*$=$ the figure on $C$ : the figure on $D$.*

*It is required to prove that*

$$A : B = C : D.$$

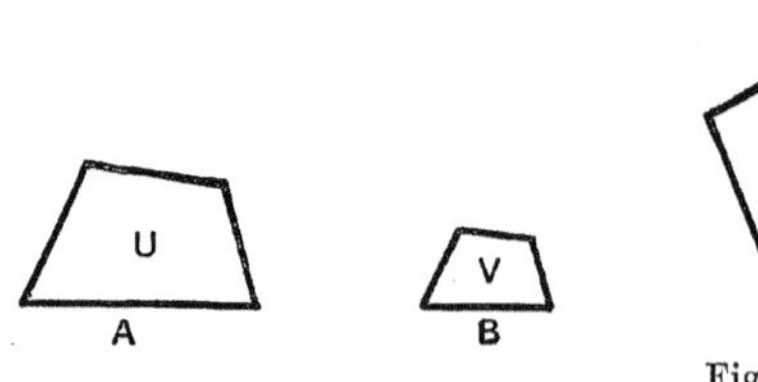


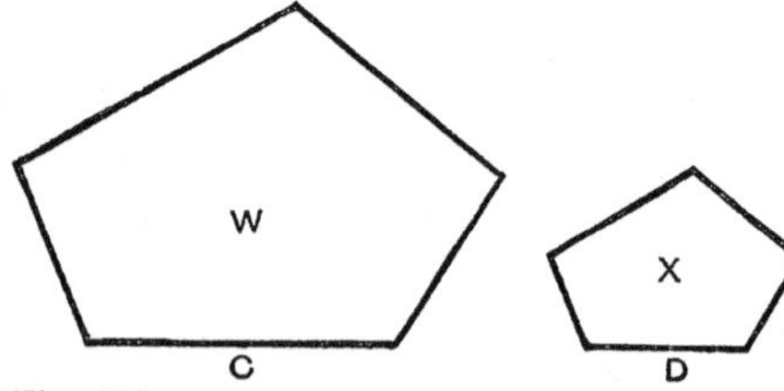


Fig. 124.

Let the similar figures on $A$ and $B$ be called $U$ and $V$ respectively.

Then $U : V =$ the square on $A$ : the square on $B$. [Art. 156.

Let the similar figures on $C$ and $D$ be called $W$ and $X$ respectively.

Then $W : X =$ the square on $C$ : the square on $D$. [Art. 156.

It is given that $U : V = W : X$,

$\therefore$ the square on $A$ : the square on $B$

$=$ the square on $C$ : the square on $D$.

If possible let $A : B$ be not equal to $C : D$.

Take $E$ so that $A : B = C : E$, [Prop. 14.

$\therefore$ the duplicate ratio of $A : B$

$=$ the duplicate ratio of $C : E$, [Prop. 37.

$\therefore$ the square on $A$ : the square on $B$

$=$ the square on $C$ : the square on $E$, [Art. 147 (2).

$\therefore$ the square on $C$ : the square on $D$

$=$ the square on $C$ : the square on $E$,

$\therefore$ the square on $D =$ the square on $E$. [Prop. 21.

But if two squares are equal, their sides must be equal.

$\therefore D = E$.

$\therefore A : B = C : D$.

## Art. 159. PROPOSITION XLVI. (Euc. VI. 31.)*

ENUNCIATION. *In any right-angled triangle, any rectilineal figure described on the hypotenuse is equal to the sum of the two similar and similarly described figures on the sides.*

Let $ABC$ be a triangle right-angled at $C$.

On $AB$ let any rectilineal figure $X$ be described.

On $BC$ let a rectilineal figure $Y$ be described similar to $X$ so that the side $BC$ of $Y$ corresponds to the side $AB$ of $X$; and on $AC$ let a rectilineal figure $Z$ be described similar to $X$ so that the side $AC$ of $Z$ corresponds to the side $AB$ of $X$.

It is required to prove that

$$X = Y + Z.$$

* I am indebted to Mr H. M. Taylor, the author of the Pitt Press Euclid, and to the Syndicate of the Pitt Press for their kind permission to use this proof, which is substantially the same as that given in the Pitt Press Euclid.

Since $X$ and $Y$ are similar figures, and $AB$, $BC$ are corresponding sides, therefore by the corollary to Proposition 44

$$X : Y = \text{square on } AB : \text{square on } BC.$$

In like manner

$$X : Z = \text{square on } AB : \text{square on } AC.$$

Now $X$, $Y$, $Z$ and the squares on $AB$, $BC$, $CA$ are all magnitudes of the same kind, viz. areas.

Fig. 125.

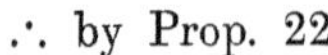

$\therefore$ by Prop. 22

$$X : \text{square on } AB = Y : \text{square on } BC,$$

and $X : \text{square on } AB = Z : \text{square on } AC,$

$\therefore\ Y : \text{square on } BC = Z : \text{square on } AC.$ [Prop. 10.

$\therefore\ Y : \text{square on } BC = Y + Z : \text{square on } BC + \text{square on } AC$ [Prop. 43.

$= Y + Z : \text{square on } AB.$

$\therefore\ X : \text{square on } AB = Y + Z : \text{square on } AB.$

$\therefore\ X = Y + Z.$ [Prop. 21.

### Art. 160. EXAMPLE 72.

In an acute-angled triangle similar figures are similarly described on the sides, show that the sum of any two of them is greater than the third.

### Art. 161. PROPOSITION XLVII. (Euc. VI. 25.)

ENUNCIATION. *To describe a rectilineal figure similar to one given rectilineal figure and equal in area to another given rectilineal figure.*

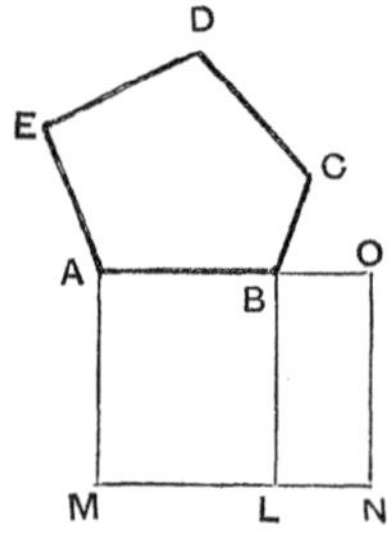


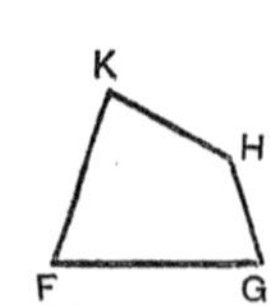


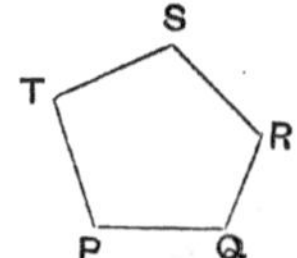


Fig. 126.

(In ordinary language to describe a figure having the shape of one given figure and the size of another.)

Let it be required to describe a figure similar to the figure *ABCDE* and equal to the figure *FGHK*.

On *AB* describe a rectangle *ABLM* equal to *ABCDE*.

On *BL* describe a rectangle *BLNO* equal to *FGHK*.

Take *PQ* a mean proportional between *AB* and *BO*. [Prop. 33.

On *PQ* describe a figure *PQRST* similar to *ABCDE*, so that *PQ* may correspond to *AB*. [Prop. 30.

It will be shewn that *PQRST* is the figure required.

Since $AB : PQ = PQ : BO$,

$\therefore$ $AB : BO$ is the duplicate ratio of $AB : PQ$. [Prop. 36.

Now $AB : BO = ABLM : BLNO$ [Prop. 17.

$= ABCDE : FGHK$.

Also the duplicate ratio of $AB : PQ = ABCDE : PQRST$. [Prop. 44.

$\therefore$ $ABCDE : FGHK = ABCDE : PQRST$.

$\therefore$ $FGHK = PQRST$. [Prop. 21.

Hence *PQRST* is equal to *FGHK* and similar to *ABCDE*.

It is therefore the figure required.

### Art. 162. *Def.* 26. FIGURES WITH SIDES RECIPROCALLY PROPORTIONAL.

**A figure is said to have the two sides about one angle reciprocally proportional to the two sides about an angle of another figure when these four sides are proportional in the following manner:**

**a side of the first figure : a side of the second figure**

**= the other side of the second figure : the other side of the first figure.**

### Art. 163. PROPOSITION XLVIII. (i). (Euc. VI. 14, 1st Part.)

ENUNCIATION. *Parallelograms having equal areas and having one angle of the one equal to one angle of the other have the sides about the equal angles reciprocally proportional.*

Let the two parallelograms be placed so that the equal angles have the same vertex, and the sides of one at that vertex lie on the sides of the other at that vertex produced.

When the parallelograms have been so placed let them be $ABCD$, $BEFG$, having the angles $A\hat{B}C$, $E\hat{B}G$ equal; and let $BE$ be on $AB$ produced, and $BG$ on $CB$ produced.

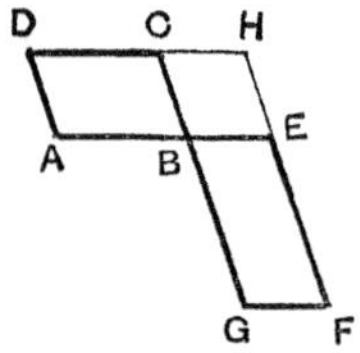

Complete the parallelogram $BEHC$.

Since $$ABCD = BEFG,$$

$$\therefore\ ABCD : BEHC = BEFG : BEHC. \quad \text{[Prop. 20.}$$

But $$ABCD : BEHC = AB : BE \quad \text{[Prop. 17.}$$

and $$BEFG : BEHC = GB : BC. \quad \text{[Prop. 17.}$$

$$\therefore\ AB : BE = BG : BC. \quad \text{[Prop. 10.}$$

Fig. 127.

Hence the two sides of $ABCD$ meeting at $B$ are reciprocally proportional to the two sides of $BEFG$ meeting at $B$.

## Art. 164. PROPOSITION XLVIII. (ii). (Euc. VI. 14, 2nd Part.)

ENUNCIATION. *Parallelograms having one angle of the one equal to one angle of the other, and the sides about the equal angles reciprocally proportional are equal in area.*

With the same figure as that in the first part of the proposition, let the parallelograms $ABCD$, $BEFG$ have

$$A\hat{B}C = E\hat{B}G,$$

and $$AB : BE = BG : BC.$$

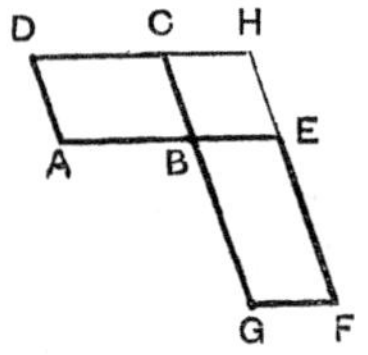

It is required to prove that $ABCD = BEFG$.

$$AB : BE = ABCD : BEHC \quad \text{[Prop. 17.}$$

and $$BG : BC = BEFG : BEHC. \quad \text{[Prop. 17.}$$

$$\therefore\ ABCD : BEHC = BEFG : BEHC,$$

$$\therefore\ ABCD = BEFG. \quad \text{[Prop. 21.}$$

Fig. 128.

### Art. 165. NOTE.

The proof of the second part of Proposition 48 is obtained by writing the steps of the proof of the first part in reverse order.

### Art. 166. PROPOSITION XLIX. (Euc. VI. 15.)

ENUNCIATION (i). *Two triangles having equal areas and having one angle of the one equal to one angle of the other have their sides about the equal angles reciprocally proportional.*

(ii) *Two triangles which have one angle in the one equal to one angle in the other and the sides about the equal angles reciprocally proportional are equal in area.*

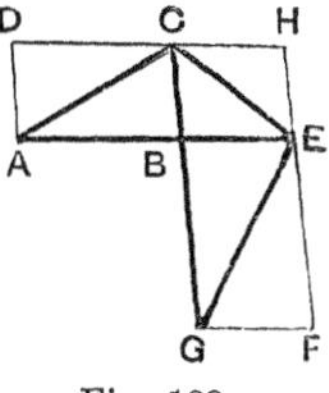

Fig. 129.

These propositions may be deduced from Proposition 48.

For the parallelograms *ABCD, BEFG, BEHC* are the doubles of the triangles *ABC, BEG, BEC* respectively; and it is merely necessary to repeat the proofs of Prop. 48, substituting for each parallelogram the triangle which is its half.

### Art. 167. EXAMPLES.

**73.** Triangles which have one angle in the one supplementary to one angle in the other and their sides about the supplementary angles reciprocally proportional are equal in area.

**74.** Triangles having equal areas and having one angle of the one supplementary to one angle of the other, have their sides about the supplementary angles reciprocally proportional.

**75.** If $P$ be any point on the side $AC$ of the triangle $ABC$, and if $PQ$ be drawn parallel to $BC$ to cut $AB$ at $Q$, then if a straight line through $P$ cut $BA$ produced through $A$ at $R$ and $BC$ at $S$ so as to make the triangles $ABC$, $BRS$ equal, prove that $QR$ will be a third proportional to $QA$ and $QB$.

**76.** The triangles $ABC$, $DEF$ are similar, and on $DE$ the side corresponding to $AB$ a point $K$ is taken so that $DK$ is a third proportional to $DE$ and $AB$, prove that the triangles $ABC$, $DKF$ are equal in area.

(This is the proposition on which Euclid's proof that similar triangles are to one another in the duplicate ratio of corresponding sides is based.)

**77.** If a straight line $DE$ be drawn parallel to the base $BC$ of the triangle $ABC$ cutting $AB$ at $D$ and $AC$ at $E$, and if $AF$ be drawn perpendicular to $DE$, prove that the rectangle $AF$, $BC$ is double of the triangle $AEB$.

# SECTION IX.

MISCELLANEOUS GEOMETRICAL PROPOSITIONS. Props. 50—55.

### Art. 168. PROPOSITION L.

ENUNCIATION. *If the vertical angle of a triangle be bisected by a straight line which also cuts the base, the rectangle contained by the sides of the triangle is equal to the rectangle contained by the segments of the base together with the square on the straight line which bisects the angle.*

Let $ABC$ be the triangle.

Bisect $B\hat{A}C$ by $AD$ cutting the base $BC$ at $D$.

It is required to prove that

rect. $AB.AC =$ rect. $BD.DC +$ square on $AD$.

Describe a circle round the triangle $ABC$, and let $AD$ cut the circle at $E$.

Join $CE$.

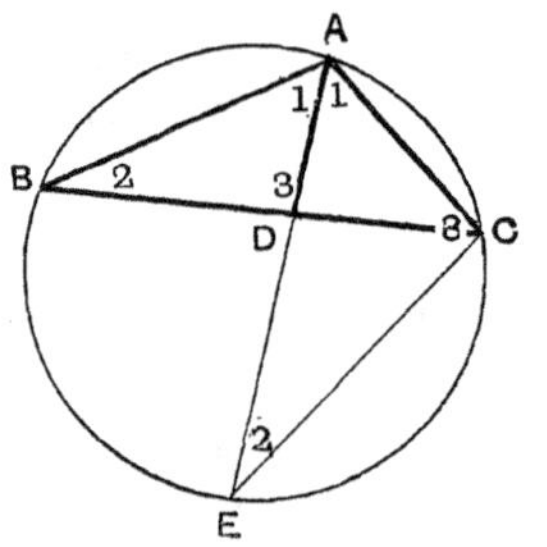

Fig. 130.

In the triangles $ABD$, $AEC$

$$B\hat{A}D = E\hat{A}C$$

$A\hat{B}D = A\hat{E}C$, since they stand on the same arc $AC$.

$$\therefore\ A\hat{D}B = A\hat{C}E.$$

Hence the triangles are similar. [Prop. 26.

$$\therefore\ BD : EC = DA : CA = AB : AE.$$

From the second and third ratios

rect. $AB.AC =$ rect $AD.AE$ [Prop. 38.

$=$ square on $AD +$ rect. $AD.DE$

$=$ square on $AD +$ rect. $BD.DC$.

### Art. 169. PROPOSITION LI.

ENUNCIATION. *If from any vertex of a triangle a perpendicular be drawn to the opposite side, the diameter of the circle circumscribing the triangle is a fourth proportional to the perpendicular and the sides of the triangle which meet at that vertex.*

Let $ABC$ be a triangle.

Let $BD$ be perpendicular to $AC$.

Let a circle be circumscribed about $ABC$.

Let $BE$ be the diameter through $B$.

Join $CE$.

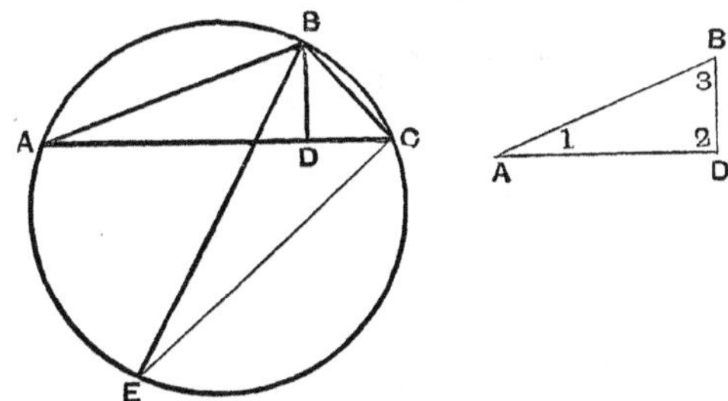


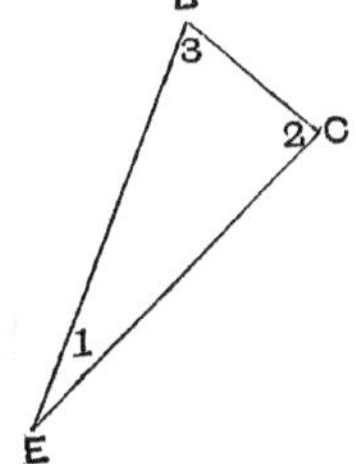


Fig. 131.

In the triangles $ABD$, $EBC$

$$B\hat{E}C = B\hat{A}D, \text{ for they stand on the same arc } BC.$$

$$B\hat{C}E = B\hat{D}A, \text{ for each is a right angle.}$$

$$\therefore\ C\hat{B}E = A\hat{B}D.$$

Hence by Prop. 26 the triangles are similar.

$$\therefore\ DB : CB = BA : BE = AD : EC.$$

From the equality of the first and second ratios it follows that the diameter $BE$ is a fourth proportional to the perpendicular $BD$ and the sides $BC$, $BA$.

### Art. 170. EXAMPLE 78.

If $D$ is any point on the side $BC$ of a triangle $ABC$, then the diameters of the circles circumscribing the triangles $ABD$ and $ACD$ are proportional to the sides $AB$, $AC$.

## Art. 171. PROPOSITION LII. (Euc. VI. 30.)

ENUNCIATION. *To divide internally or externally a finite straight line in extreme and mean ratio;* i.e. so that the whole line is to one segment as that segment is to the other segment.

Let $AB$ be the straight line, it is required to find a point $C$ on it so that

$$AB : AC = AC : CB.$$

On $AB$ describe the square $ABDE$.

Bisect $AE$ at $F$.

Join $FB$.

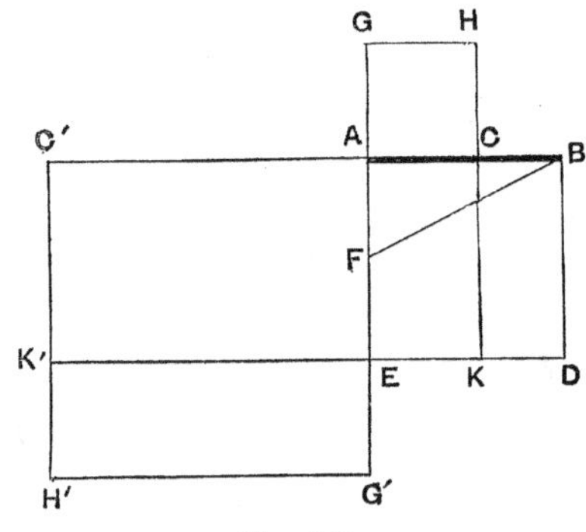


Fig. 132.

On $EFA$ measure $FG = FG' = FB$.

On $AG$ describe the square $ACHG$.

On $AG'$ describe the square $AC'H'G'$.

The points $C$, $C'$ fall on $AB$, and are the required points.

It is proved in Prop. 11 of the Second Book of Euclid that

the square on $AC =$ rect. $AB.BC$.

$\therefore\ AB : AC = AC : BC.$ [Cor. to Prop. 38.

To prove the same property for the point $C'$.

Since $AE$ is bisected at $F$ and produced to $G'$,

$\therefore$ square on $FG' =$ square on $FA +$ rect. $EG'.AG'$.

$\therefore$ square on $FB =$ square on $FA +$ rect. $EG'H'K'$.

$\therefore$ square on $FA$ + square on $AB$ = square on $FA$ + rect. $EG'H'K'$.

$\therefore$ square on $AB$ = rect. $EG'H'K'$.

$$\therefore\ AEDB = EG'H'K'.$$

$$\therefore\ AEDB + AEK'C' = EG'H'K' + AEK'C'.$$

$$\therefore\ BDK'C' \qquad = AC'H'G'.$$

$\therefore$ rect. $BA \,.\, BC'$ = square on $AC'$.

$$\therefore\ AB : AC' = AC' : C'B.$$ [Cor. to Prop. 38.

### Art. 172. EXAMPLE 79.

If $ABC$ be a triangle right-angled at $A$, and $AD$ be drawn perpendicular to the hypotenuse cutting it at $D$, and if $D$ divide $BC$ in extreme and mean ratio, then prove that the sides of the triangle $ABC$ are in proportion.

## Art. 173. PROPOSITION LIII. (Euc. VI. 24.)

ENUNCIATION. *Parallelograms about the diagonal of any parallelogram are similar to the whole and to one another.*

Let $ABCD$ be a parallelogram.

Let $AEFH$, $FKCG$ be parallelograms about the diagonal $AC$ of the parallelogram $ABCD$.

It is required to prove that they are similar to $ABCD$ and to one another.

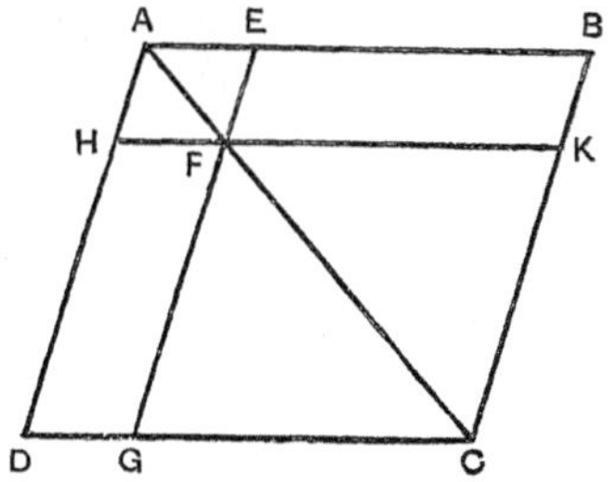

Since $EF$ is parallel to $BC$,
the triangles $AEF$, $ABC$ are similar. [Cor. to Prop. 26.

$$\therefore\ AE : AB = EF : BC = FA : CA.$$

Since $FH$ is parallel to $CD$,
the triangles $AFH$, $ACD$ are similar. [Cor. to Prop. 26.

Fig. 133.

$$\therefore\ FA : CA = AH : AD = HF : DC.$$

Hence $AE : AB = EF : BC = FH : CD = HA : DA$. [Prop. 10.

Further

$$H\hat{A}E = D\hat{A}B,$$
$$A\hat{E}F = A\hat{B}C,$$
$$E\hat{F}H = B\hat{C}D,$$
$$F\hat{H}A = C\hat{D}A.$$

Hence the two sets of conditions for the similarity of $AEFH$, $ABCD$ are satisfied (Art. 91).

In like manner $FKCG$ is similar to $ABCD$.

$\therefore$ $AEFH$, $FKCG$ are similar. [Prop. 25.

### Art. 174. PROPOSITION LIV. (Euc. VI. 26.)

ENUNCIATION. *If two similar parallelograms have a common angle and be similarly situated they are about the same diagonal.*

Let $ABCD$, $AEFH$ be two similar parallelograms having the same angle $A$. Let them be similarly situated, and let $AB$, $AE$ be corresponding sides.

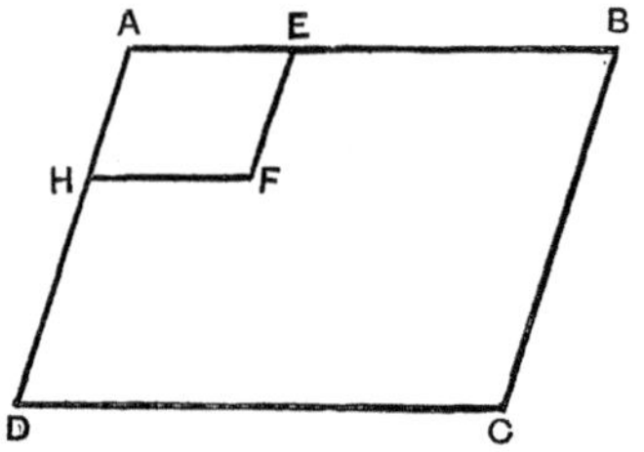

It is required to prove that the diagonals $AC$, $AF$ coincide in direction.

Since the parallelograms are similar

$$A\hat{B}C = A\hat{E}F,$$

$$AB : AE = BC : EF.$$

$$\therefore \; AB : BC = AE : EF. \qquad \text{[Prop. 22.}$$

Fig. 134.

Hence the triangles $ABC$, $AEF$ are similar. [Prop. 28.

In these triangles $BC$, $EF$ are corresponding sides.

Hence the angles opposite them are equal.

$$\therefore \; B\hat{A}C = E\hat{A}F.$$

Hence $AC$ coincides in direction with $AF$.

Hence the parallelograms $ABCD$, $AEFH$ are about the same diagonal.

### Art. 175. EXAMPLE 80.

Let the straight line $AB$ be produced through $A$ to $P$ and through $B$ to $Q$, so that $AP$ is equal to $BQ$. On $BQ$, $BP$ let similar parallelograms be similarly described, viz. $BQRS$ and $BPTU$. Prove that the parallelogram whose adjacent sides are $QA$, $QR$ is equal to that whose adjacent sides are $PA$, $PT$.

## Art. 176. PROPOSITION LV. (Euc. VI. 27, 28, 29.)

ENUNCIATION. *If $OAB$ be a given triangle it is required to find a point $P$ on $AB$ or $AB$ produced so that if $PQ$ be drawn parallel to $OB$ to cut $OA$ in $Q$, and if $PR$ be drawn parallel to $OA$ to cut $OB$ in $R$, then the parallelogram $PQOR$ may have a given area.*

There are two kinds of cases.

**Case I.** Suppose the point $P$ to have been found and to lie between $A$ and $F$, the middle point of $AB$.

Let $E$ be the middle point of $OA$.

Complete the parallelogram $EAVF$.

Let $QP$ cut $FV$ in $T$.

Let $PR$ cut $EF$ in $S$ and $AV$ in $U$.

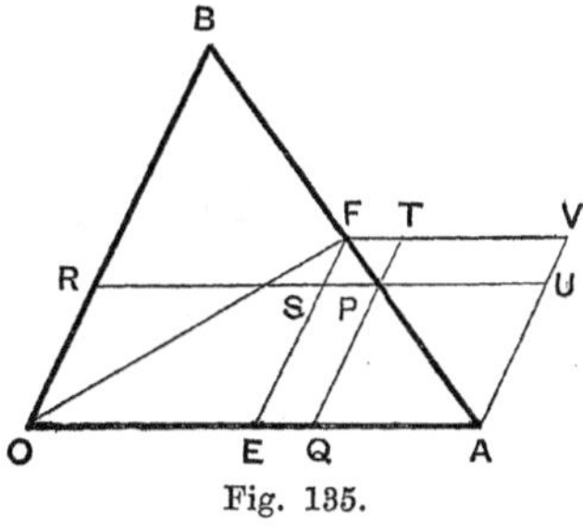

Fig. 135.

Then $OQPR = OESR + EQPS$

$= EAUS + PUVT$

$= EAVF - SPTF$

$= \triangle OAF - SPTF.$

Hence if $P$ be between $A$ and $F$ the area $OQPR$ is less than the triangle $OAF$. (This is equivalent to the result of Euc. VI. 27.)

Hence $SPTF = \triangle OAF - OQPR$

$= \frac{1}{2}$(given triangle $OAB$) $-$ (a given area).

Hence the parallelogram $SPTF$ has a known area.

It is also known to be similar to the known parallelogram $EAVF$.

Hence it can be constructed by Prop. 47, and if it be placed so that the side corresponding to $FV$ falls along $FV$, and the side corresponding to $FE$ falls along $FE$, then its diagonal will fall on $FA$ by Prop. 54.

Hence the position of $P$ is known.

(This is equivalent to the result of Euc. VI. 28.)

In order that the construction for $P$ may be possible it is necessary that the given area should not exceed half the given triangle $OAB$.

The above construction applies only to the case where $P$ lies between $A$ and $F$, the middle point of $AB$.

If $P$ be one position of the required point, let a point $P'$ be taken on $FB$ so that $PF = P'F$, and let $Q'$, $R'$, $S'$, $T'$ be the points corresponding to $Q$, $R$, $S$, $T$.

Then the parallelograms $SPTF$, $S'P'T'F$ are equal.

Hence the parallelograms $OQPR$, $OQ'P'R'$ are equal.

Hence $P'$ is another position of the required point.

**Case II.** Let $P$ be on $BA$ produced through $A$, and let the same construction be made.

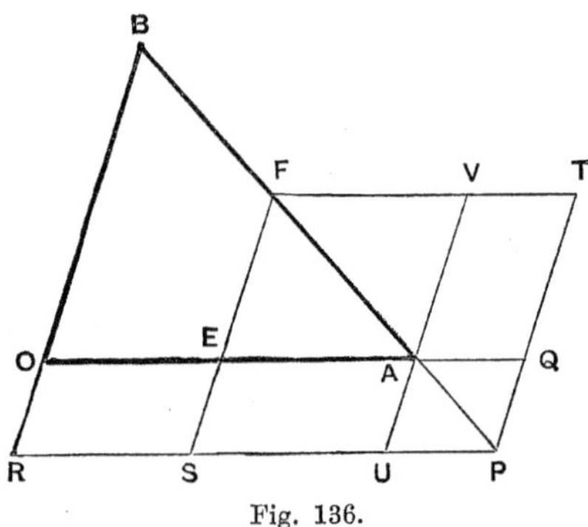


Fig. 136.

Then
$$\begin{aligned} OQPR &= OESR + EQPS \\ &= EAUS + PUVT \\ &= SPTF - EAVF \\ &= SPTF - \triangle OAF. \\ \therefore\ SPTF &= \triangle OAF + OQPR \\ &= \tfrac{1}{2}(\text{given triangle } OAB) + (\text{a given area}). \end{aligned}$$

Hence the parallelogram $SPTF$ has a known area.

It is also known to be similar to the known parallelogram $EAVF$.

Hence it can be constructed by Prop. 47, and if it be placed so that the side corresponding to $FV$ falls along $FV$, and the side corresponding to $FE$ falls along $FE$, then its diagonal will fall along $FA$ by Prop. 54.

Hence the position of $P$ is known.

(This is equivalent to the result of Euc. VI. 29.)

In this case the construction is always possible for all magnitudes of the given area.

If $P$ be one position of the required point, and a point $P'$ be taken on $FB$ produced through $B$ so that $P'F = PF$, then it may be shown that $P'$ is another position of the required point.

It results from Cases I and II that if the given area be less than half the given triangle $OAB$ there are *four* solutions of the problem, viz. $P$ may be between $A$ and $F$ or between $F$ and $B$, or on $BA$ produced through $A$, or on $AB$ produced through $B$.

If the given area be equal to half the triangle $OAB$ there are *three* solutions, viz. $P$ may be at $F$, or on $BA$ produced through $A$, or on $AB$ produced through $B$.

If the given area be greater than half the triangle $OAB$ there are *two* solutions, viz. $P$ may be on $BA$ produced through $A$, or on $AB$ produced through $B$.

# SECTION X.

THE REMAINING IMPORTANT PROPOSITIONS IN THE THEORY OF SCALES AND OF RATIOS, WITH GEOMETRICAL APPLICATIONS. Props. 56–63.

### Art. 177. PROPOSITION LVI.* (Euc. V. 23.)

ENUNCIATION 1.

If $A$, $B$, $C$ are three magnitudes of the same kind,
if $T$, $U$, $V$ are three magnitudes of the same kind,
if $A : B = U : V$,
and $B : C = T : U$,
prove that $A : C = T : V$.

ENUNCIATION 2.

*If $A$, $B$, $C$ are three magnitudes of the same kind,*
*if $T$, $U$, $V$ are three magnitudes of the same kind,*
*if* $[A, B] \simeq [U, V]$,
*if* $[B, C] \simeq [T, U]$,
*prove that* $[A, C] \simeq [T, V]$.

As in Props. 22 and 35 it is best to make use of the second form of the conditions in Prop. 8 and it is necessary to show that

(1) If $rA < sC$, then $rT < sV$,

(2) If $rA > sC$, then $rT > sV$,

(3) If $rT < sV$, then $rA < sC$,

(4) If $rT > sV$, then $rA > sC$.

* See Note 11.

If
$$rA < sC,$$
then integers $n$, $t$ exist such that
$$nrA < tB,$$
and
$$tB < nsC. \qquad \text{[Prop. 7.}$$
$$\because\ nrA < tB$$
the scale of $A$, $B$ shows the fact exhibited in Fig. 137.

But
$$[A, B] \simeq [U, V].$$
Hence the scale of $U$, $V$ shows the fact exhibited in Fig. 138.
$$\therefore\ nrU < tV \ \ldots\ldots\ldots\ldots\ldots\ldots\ldots\ldots\ldots \text{(I)}.$$
Again
$$\because\ tB < nsC,$$
the scale of $B$, $C$ shows the fact exhibited in Fig. 139.

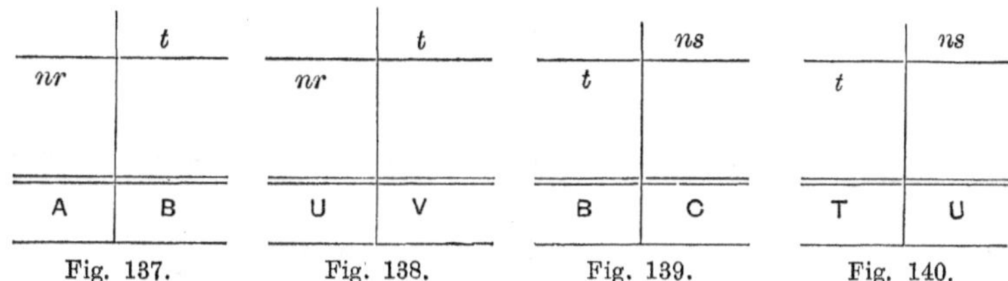


Fig. 137. Fig. 138. Fig. 139. Fig. 140.

But
$$[B, C] \simeq [T, U].$$
Hence the scale of $T$, $U$ shows the fact exhibited in Fig. 140.
$$\therefore\ tT < nsU \ldots\ldots\ldots\ldots\ldots\ldots\ldots\ldots\ldots \text{(II)*}.$$
From (I)
$$snrU < stV.$$
From (II)
$$rtT < rnsU.$$
Now
$$snrU = rnsU.$$
$$\therefore\ rtT < stV.$$
$$\therefore\ rT < sV.$$
$$\therefore \text{ if } rA < sC, \text{ then } rT < sV \ldots\ldots\ldots\ldots\ldots\ldots \text{(III)}.$$
In like manner
$$\text{if } rA > sC, \text{ then } rT > sV \ldots\ldots\ldots\ldots\ldots\ldots \text{(IV)},$$
$$\text{if } rT < sV, \text{ then } rA < sC \ldots\ldots\ldots\ldots\ldots\ldots \text{(V)},$$
$$\text{if } rT > sV, \text{ then } rA > sC \ldots\ldots\ldots\ldots\ldots\ldots \text{(VI)}.$$
From (III), (IV), (V), (VI) it follows by Prop. 8 that
$$[A, C] \simeq [T, V].$$

* The result required is an algebraic consequence of the inequalities (I) and (II), and is obtained by so transforming them that the multiples of $U$ become the same in each.

## Art. 178. NOTE.

The proof of (IV) follows from that of (III) by reversing all the signs of inequality, and making the corresponding changes in the figures.

To get (V), if $rT < sV$, then integers $n$, $t$ exist by Prop. 7 such that

$$nrT < tU$$

and

$$tU < nsV.$$

Now proceed as in the proof of (III).

Or else observe that the given conditions

$$[A, B] \simeq [U, V]$$

and

$$[B, C] \simeq [T, U]$$

are equivalent to

$$[V, U] \simeq [B, A]$$

$$[U, T] \simeq [C, B].$$

Hence they are obtainable from the original conditions by interchanging

$A$ and $V$, $B$ and $U$, $C$ and $T$.

Making these changes in (III) and also interchanging $r$ and $s$, which is permissible since $r$ and $s$ are any integers, it will be found that (VI) results; in like manner (IV) gives (V).

## Art. 179. EXAMPLES.

**81.** Using the symbol $\divideontimes$ as an abbreviation for the words "compounded with," prove that

(i) $$(A : B) \divideontimes (C : D) = (C : D) \divideontimes (A : B).$$

(ii) $$[(A : B) \divideontimes (C : D)] \divideontimes (E : F)$$
$$= (A : B) \divideontimes [(C : D) \divideontimes (E : F)].$$

**82.** Prove that $(A : B) \divideontimes [(B : A) \divideontimes (C : D)] = C : D.$

Hence show how to find the ratio which must be compounded with $A : B$ to give the ratio $C : D$.

**83.** Prove that $[(A : B) \divideontimes (C : D)] \divideontimes (D : C) = (A : B).$

**84.** If

$$E : C = A : P$$

$$E : D = B : Q,$$

prove that

$$(A : B) \divideontimes (C : D) = (P : Q).$$

**85.** What is the result of compounding any ratio with a ratio of equality? What is the result of compounding a ratio of equality with any ratio?

**86.** If a ratio be compounded with its reciprocal show that the result is a ratio of equality.

**87.** If $A$, $B$, $C$, $D$ be magnitudes all of the same kind, prove that

$$A : B \text{ compounded with } C : D$$

gives the same result as

$$A : D \text{ compounded with } C : B.$$

**88.** Prove that $A : B$ compounded with $C : D$ gives $L : B$ where $D : C = A : L$.

**89.** If $A$, $B$, $C$, $D$ are all magnitudes of the same kind, and

$$D : A \text{ compounded with } D : B$$

is equal to $D : C$, find the relation between $A$, $B$, $C$, $D$.

If $A$, $B$, $C$, $D$ are all magnitudes of the same kind, and if $A : D$ compounded with $B : D$ give $C : D$, find the relation between $A$, $B$, $C$, $D$.

**90.** (i) What ratio must be compounded with $A : C$ to give $B : C$?

(ii) What ratio must be compounded with $C : A$ to give $C : B$?

**91.** If the duplicate ratio of $A : B$ be equal to the duplicate ratio of $C : D$, then prove that $A : B = C : D$.

**92.** (i) Prove the theorem of Menelaus; viz. if a straight line $A'B'C'$ cut the sides of the triangle $ABC$, viz. $BC$ in $A'$, $CA$ in $B'$, $AB$ in $C'$; then the ratio compounded of the ratios

$$BA' : A'C, \quad CB' : B'A, \quad AC' : C'B$$

is a ratio of equality.

(ii) Prove the converse of the theorem of Menelaus: if the sides of the triangle $A'B'C'$ be divided, $BC$ in $A'$, $CA$ in $B'$, $AB$ in $C'$, so that two of the points of division are internal and one external, or else all three are external; and if further the ratio compounded of

$$BA' : A'C, \quad CB' : B'A, \quad AC' : C'B$$

is a ratio of equality, then the points $A'$, $B'$, $C'$ lie on one straight line.

**93.** Prove that the six centres of similitude* of three circles lie three by three on four straight lines (called the axes of similitude of the circles).

[Apply the last example, taking $A$, $B$, $C$ at the centres of the circles.]

**94.** (i) Prove the theorem of Ceva, viz.:

If $O$ be a point in the plane of the triangle $ABC$, if $AO$ cut $BC$ at $A'$, if

* See Ex. 40.

$BO$ cut $CA$ at $B'$, if $CO$ cut $AB$ at $C'$, then the ratio compounded of $BA' : A'C$, $CB' : B'A$, $AC' : C'B$ is a ratio of equality.

(ii) Prove the converse of the theorem of Ceva, viz.:

If the sides of the triangle $ABC$ be divided, $BC$ at $A'$, $CA$ at $B'$, $AB$ at $C'$, so that two of the points of division are external and one internal, or else all three are internal, and if further the ratio compounded of $BA' : A'C$, $CB' : B'A$, $AC' : C'B$ is a ratio of equality, then the three straight lines $AA'$, $BB'$, $CC'$ are concurrent.

### **Art. 180.** *Def.* 27. CROSS OR ANHARMONIC RATIO.

**If $A$, $B$, $C$, $D$ be four points on a straight line, they determine six segments on that line.**

**Take any one of these six segments, say $BD$.**

**Then $A$ divides it in the ratio $AB : AD$; and $C$ divides it in the ratio $CB : CD$.**

**Then the ratio which must be compounded with either of these ratios to produce the other is *a* value of the cross or anharmonic ratio of the four points*.**

### **Art. 181.** EXAMPLES.

95. If $A$, $B$, $C$, $D$ be four points on a straight line, and $O$ any point not on that straight line, and if through $B$ a straight line be drawn parallel to $OD$ to cut $OA$ at $E$ and $OC$ at $F$, then prove that

$$(CB : CD) \ast (BE : BF) = (AB : AD).$$

96. By means of the preceding example prove that if four fixed straight lines passing through a point be cut by *any* fifth straight line, then the cross-ratio of the four points of intersection is independent of the position of the fifth straight line.

97. If $A_1$, $B_1$, $C_1$ be any three points on a straight line; and $A_2$, $B_2$, $C_2$ any three points on another straight line, show how to determine points $D_1$, $D_2$ on the two straight lines so that the cross-ratio of $A_1$, $B_1$, $C_1$, $D_1$ shall be equal to that of $A_2$, $B_2$, $C_2$, $D_2$. [On the straight line $A_1A_2$ take any two points $O_1$, $O_2$. Let $O_1B_1$, $O_2B_2$ meet at $B$; let $O_1C_1$, $O_2C_2$ meet at $C$; then show that the points $D_1$, $D_2$ are such that $O_1D_1$, $O_2D_2$ intersect on $BC$.]

* This definition is sufficient for solving the problems set in this book. It is not however a complete one as the signs of the segments have not been specified. When the signs are specified, it can be shown that there are six values of the cross ratio, all of which are determined when any one is given.

**98.** If $ABC$ be a triangle, if $D$ be the middle point of $BC$, if any straight line through $D$ cut $AB$ at $E$, $AC$ at $F$, and a parallel through $A$ to $BC$ at $G$, then find the value of the cross-ratio of $E$, $D$, $F$, $G$.

**99.** If $A$, $B$, $C$, $D$ be four fixed points on a circle, and $P$, $Q$ any two other points on the same circle, prove that the cross-ratio of the four straight lines $PA$, $PB$, $PC$, $PD$ is equal to that of the four straight lines $QA$, $QB$, $QC$, $QD$; and also to that of the four points in which the tangent at $P$ to the circle is cut by the tangents at $A$, $B$, $C$, $D$.

**100.** Let the points $P$, $P'$ on the straight line $OX$ be said to correspond when the rectangle $OP.OP'$ is equal to a given rectangle. Then prove that the cross-ratio of any four points is equal to the cross-ratio of their corresponding points.

**101.** If from any point two tangents be drawn to a circle, the points of contact and the points of intersection of any secant from the same point are such that the straight lines joining them to any fifth point on the circle form a harmonic pencil.

**102.** (i) Through any point $O$ a tangent $OU$ and a secant $ORS$ are drawn to a circle; $OPQ$ is another secant passing through the centre of the circle ($P$, $Q$ being the extremities of a diameter). Show that if $QR$, $QU$, $QS$ cut the tangent at $P$ at $R'$, $U'$, $S'$ respectively, then

$$PR' : PU' = PU' : PS'.$$

(ii) If the point $O$ be inside the circle, and $U$ be taken as the extremity of the shortest chord through $O$, and the rest of the construction be as above, show that

$$PR' : PU' = PU' : PS'.$$

## Art. 182. PROPOSITION LVII. (Euc. V. 18.)

ENUNCIATION 1. If two ratios are equal, the ratio of the sum of the antecedent and consequent of the first ratio to the consequent of the first ratio is equal to the ratio of the sum of the antecedent and consequent of the second ratio to the consequent of the second ratio;

i.e. if $$A : B = X : Y,$$
to prove that $$A + B : B = X + Y : Y.$$

ENUNCIATION 2. *If the scale of* $A$, $B$ *is the same as that of* $X$, $Y$,
*to prove that* *the scale of* $A + B$, $B$ *is the same as that of* $X + Y$, $Y$.
*i.e. if* $$[A, B] \simeq [X, Y],$$
*to prove that* $$[A + B, B] \simeq [X + Y, Y].$$

Take any integer $r$ in the first column,
and any integer $s$ in the second column,
of the scale of $A + B$, $B$.

Then there are three alternatives indicated by the figures

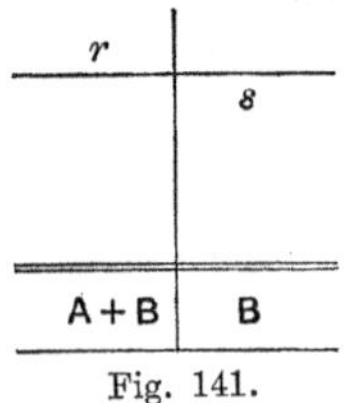

Fig. 141.

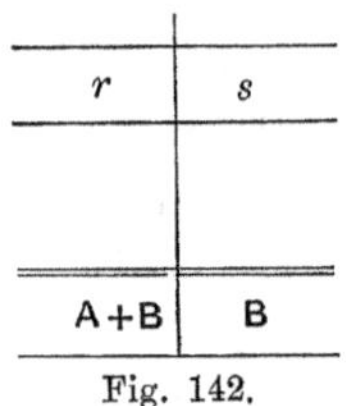

Fig. 142.

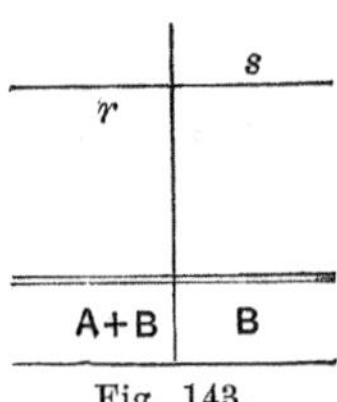

Fig. 143.

which express the facts

$$r(A + B) > sB$$

There are three alternatives

$r < s$, $r = s$, $r > s$.

If $r < s$ it can be written

$rA > (s - r) B$.

$$r(A + B) = sB$$

This is impossible unless

$r < s$.

Hence it can be written

$rA = (s - r) B$.

$$r(A + B) < sB$$

This is impossible unless

$r < s$.

Hence it can be written

$rA < (s - r) B$.

Hence in the scale of $A$, $B$ there are the figures

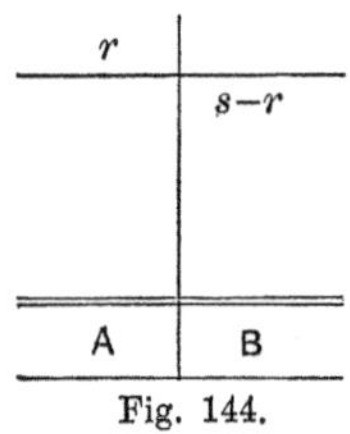

Fig. 144.

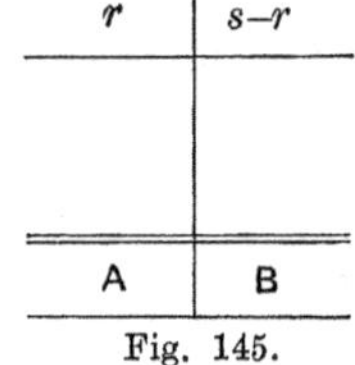

Fig. 145.

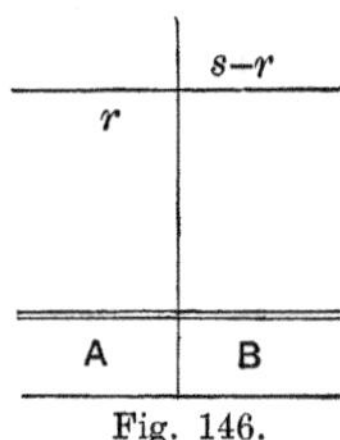

Fig. 146.

Now $$[A, B] \simeq [X, Y].$$

Hence there are the following figures

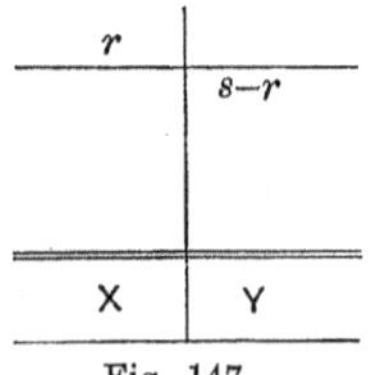

Fig. 147.

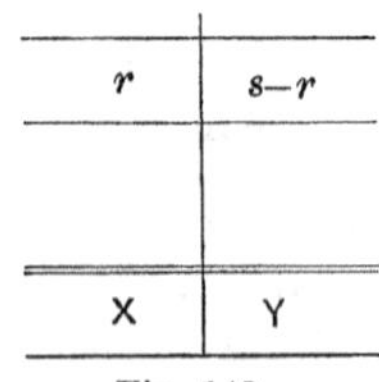

Fig. 148.

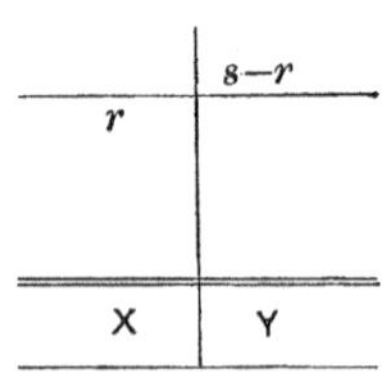

Fig. 149.

These figures indicate the facts

$$rX > (s-r)\,Y \qquad rX = (s-r)\,Y \qquad rX < (s-r)\,Y.$$

$$\therefore\ r(X+Y) > sY \qquad r(X+Y) = sY \qquad r(X+Y) < sY.$$

There remains in this case the consideration of the cases

$$r = s,\ r > s$$

in which

$$rY = sY,\ rY > sY.$$

Hence in both cases

$$r(X+Y) > sY$$

as before.

Hence there are the three figures

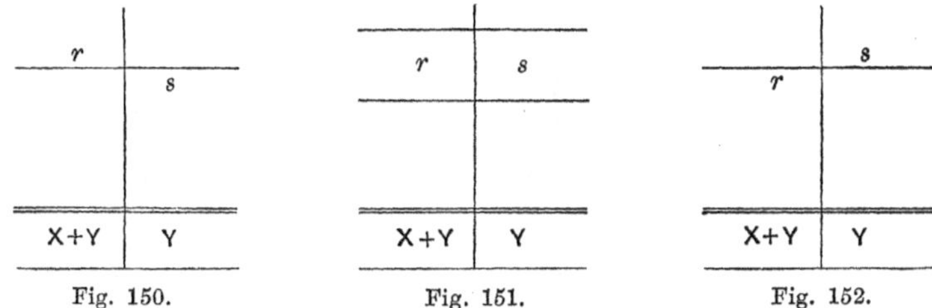


Fig. 150. Fig. 151. Fig. 152.

Comparing Figures 150, 151, 152 with Figures 141, 142, 143 respectively it follows that

$$[A+B,\ B] \simeq [X+Y,\ Y].$$

## Art. 183. EXAMPLES.

**103.** If $ABC$ be a triangle right-angled at $C$, and if $AD$ bisect the angle $BAC$ cutting $BC$ at $D$, prove that

$$AC : CD = AC + AB : BC.$$

(By means of this proposition Archimedes showed that the length of the circumference of a circle was less than $3\frac{1}{7}$ times its diameter.)

**104.** If $ABC$ be a triangle right-angled at $C$, if $AD$ bisect the angle $BAC$ and cut $BC$ at $D$, and if $BE$ be drawn perpendicular to $AD$ cutting it at $E$, prove that

$$AE : EB = AC + AB : BC.$$

(By means of this proposition Archimedes showed that the length of the circumference of a circle was greater than $3\frac{10}{71}$ times its diameter.)

## Art. 184. PROPOSITION LVIII. (Euc. V. 17.)

ENUNCIATION 1. If two ratios are equal, then the ratio of the difference of the antecedent and consequent of the first ratio to the consequent of the first ratio is equal to the ratio of the difference of the antecedent and consequent of the second ratio to the consequent of the second ratio;

i.e. if $$A : B = X : Y,$$
then $$A \sim B : B = X \sim Y : Y.$$

ENUNCIATION 2. *If* $$[A, B] \simeq [X, Y],$$
*then* $$[A \sim B, B] \simeq [X \sim Y, Y].$$

It is necessary to consider separately the cases
$$A > B,$$
$$A = B,$$
$$A < B.$$

If $A > B$, and therefore $X > Y$, then it is required to prove that
$$[A - B, B] \simeq [X - Y, Y].$$

Take any integer $r$ in the first column,
and any integer $s$ in the second column,
of the scale of $A - B$, $B$.

There are three alternatives corresponding to the figures

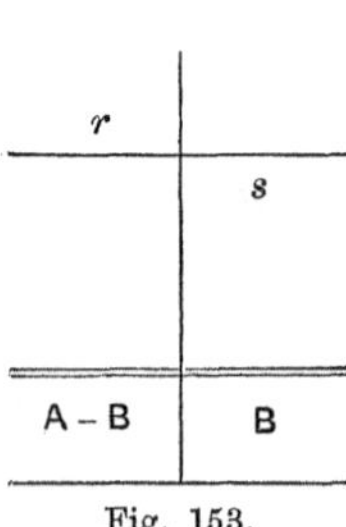

Fig. 153.

Fig. 154.

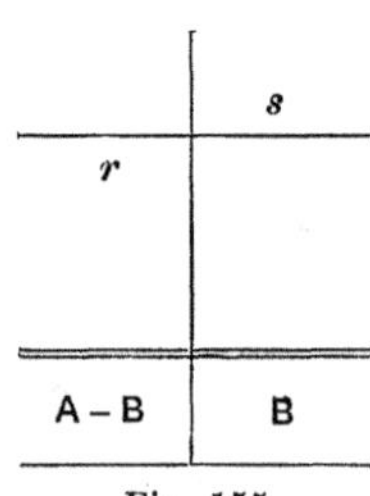

Fig. 155.

which express the facts

| | | |
|---|---|---|
| $r(A - B) > sB$ | $r(A - B) = sB$ | $r(A - B) < sB$ |
| $rA > (r + s)B$ | $rA = (r + s)B$ | $rA < (r + s)B$ |

to which correspond the figures

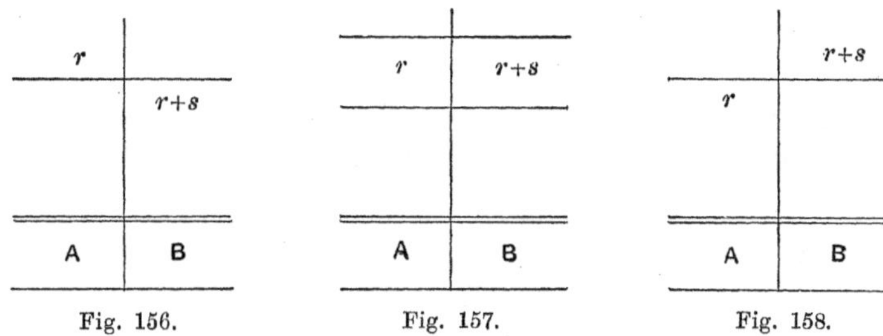


Fig. 156. Fig. 157. Fig. 158.

Now $$[A, B] \simeq [X, Y].$$

Hence there are the figures

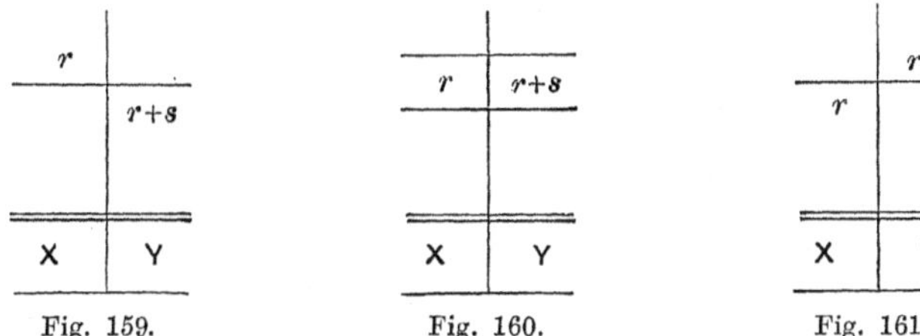


Fig. 159. Fig. 160. Fig. 161.

which correspond respectively to

$$rX > (r+s)\,Y \qquad rX = (r+s)\,Y \qquad rX < (r+s)\,Y$$

i.e. to

$$r(X-Y) > sY \qquad r(X-Y) = sY \qquad r(X-Y) < sY.$$

Hence there are the figures

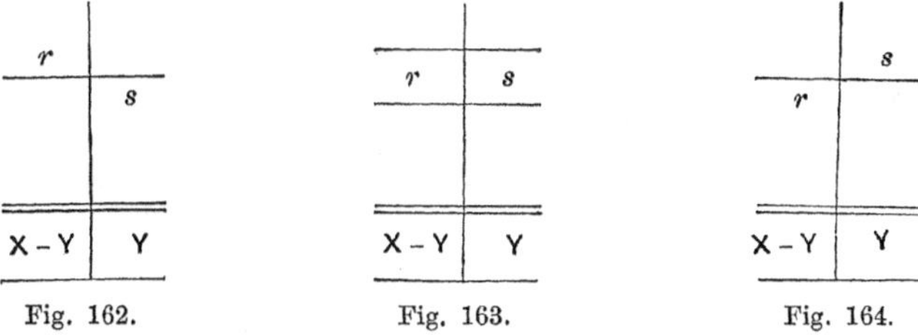


Fig. 162. Fig. 163. Fig. 164.

Comparing therefore Figs. 153, 154, 155 with Figs. 162, 163, 164 respectively it follows that

$$[A-B, B] \simeq [X-Y, Y].$$

If $A = B$, then $X = Y$.

Hence the difference of $A$ and $B$, and the difference of $X$ and $Y$, are both zero.

Hence the first term of each of the scales

$$[A \sim B, B] \text{ and } [X \sim Y, Y]$$

is zero, and the scales may be considered to be the same.

If $A < B$, and therefore $X < Y$, then it is required to show that

$$[B - A, B] \simeq [Y - X, Y].$$

This may be proved independently as in the first case, or may be deduced from it.

For if $[A, B] \simeq [X, Y]$,

then $[B, A] \simeq [Y, X]$. [Prop. 19.

$\therefore [B - A, A] \simeq [Y - X, X]$, by Case 1.

But $[A, B] \simeq [X, Y]$.

$\therefore [B - A, B] \simeq [Y - X, Y]$. [Prop. 35.

## Art. 185. EXAMPLES.

**105.** Prove the last case of Proposition 58 directly in a manner similar to that adopted for the first case.

**106.** If $A : B = X : Y$, and $A > B$, prove that

$$A : A - B = X : X - Y.$$

**107.** If $A : B = B : C$, and $A > B$, prove that

$$A - C : A - B = B + C : B.$$

## Art. 186. PROPOSITION LIX.

ENUNCIATION. *If* $A : B = X : Y$,

*prove that* $A \sim B : A + B = X \sim Y : X + Y$.

*If* $A : B = X : Y$,

*then* $A + B : B = X + Y : Y$. [Prop. 57.

$\therefore B : A + B = Y : X + Y$. [Prop. 19.

*Also* $A \sim B : B = X \sim Y : Y$. [Prop. 58.

$\therefore A \sim B : A + B = X \sim Y : X + Y$. [Prop. 35.

## Art. 187. PROPOSITION LX.

ENUNCIATION. *If $A$, $B$, $C$, $D$ be four harmonic points, $A$ and $C$ being conjugate, and if $O$ be the middle point of $AC$, then $OC$ is a mean proportional between $OB$ and $OD$.*

A O B C D

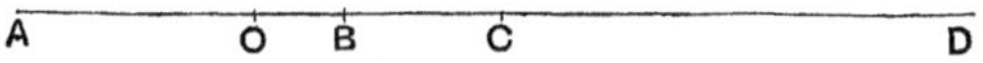

Fig. 165.

Since $A$ divides $BD$ in the same ratio as $C$ does,

$$AB : AD = BC : CD.$$

$$\therefore\ AB : BC = AD : CD.$$ [Prop. 22.

$$\therefore\ AB - BC : AB + BC = AD - CD : AD + CD.$$ [Prop. 59.

$$\therefore\ 2OB : 2OC = 2OC : 2OD.$$

$$\therefore\ OB : OC = OC : OD.$$ [Prop. 9.

$\therefore$ $OC$ is a mean proportional between $OB$ and $OD$.

## Art. 188. EXAMPLES.

**108.** Prove that if a circle be drawn through two points which are inverse with regard to a second circle, then the two circles cut each other at right angles.

**109.** If $A$, $B$, $C$, $D$ be four harmonic points, and if $O$ be the middle point of $AC$, show that a circle can be drawn with centre $O$ so as to cut at right angles any circle that can be drawn through $B$ and $D$ in the plane of the circle whose centre is $O$.

**110.** If the diagonals $AC$, $BD$ of the quadrilateral $ABCD$ intersect at $E$ and a straight line $EG$ be drawn parallel to one of the sides $AB$ meeting the opposite side $CD$ in $G$ and the third diagonal (i.e. the straight line joining $H$ the intersection of $AB$ and $CD$ to $I$ the intersection of $AD$ and $BC$) in $J$, then $EJ$ is bisected at $G$.

[If $EG$ cut $AD$ in $K$ and $BC$ in $L$, prove that

$$AB : BH = KL : LJ = EL : LG = KE : EG.]$$

Hence by the aid of Ex. 53 show that $HA$, $HE$, $HC$, $HI$ are four harmonic lines.

### Art. 189. PROPOSITION LXI. (Euc. V. 24.)

ENUNCIATION 1. If $A : C = X : Z,$

and $B : C = Y : Z,$

prove that $A + B : C = X + Y : Z.$

ENUNCIATION 2. *If* $[A, C] \simeq [X, Z],$

*and* $[B, C] \simeq [Y, Z],$

*prove that* $[A + B, C] \simeq [X + Y, Z].$

Since $[B, C] \simeq [Y, Z],$

$\therefore [C, B] \simeq [Z, Y],$ [Prop. 19.

but $[A, C] \simeq [X, Z].$

$\therefore [A, B] \simeq [X, Y].$ [Prop. 35.

$\therefore [A + B, B] \simeq [X + Y, Y],$ [Prop. 57.

but $[B, C] \simeq [Y, Z].$

$\therefore [A + B, C] \simeq [X + Y, Z].$ [Prop. 35.

**Art. 190.** On this proposition depends the process, called in this book the Aggregating of Ratios, which corresponds to the addition of the measures of the ratios.

### Art. 191. THE AGGREGATING OF RATIOS.

The development of this process is made in four stages.

STAGE 1. The general idea at the root of the process of aggregating ratios is this:—

When it is desired to find the ratio of one magnitude to a second, it is permissible to break up the first magnitude into two parts, then to find the ratio of each part to the second magnitude, and then to add the two ratios thus found.

(It should be carefully noticed that it is the first magnitude, *not the second*, which may be broken up.)

STAGE 2. To make the general idea stated in the first stage quite precise the following definition is necessary.

Let the ratio $X + Y : Z$ be said to be aggregated from the ratios $X : Z$ and $Y : Z$. It is known when the magnitudes $X$, $Y$, $Z$ are known.

(This may be compared with Euclid's 22nd Datum.)

Let the symbol $\frown$ placed between two ratios denote that they are to be aggregated.

Then $$X + Y : Z = (X : Z) \frown (Y : Z).$$

STAGE 3. In the second stage the two ratios which are aggregated both have the same second term, and therefore do not at first sight appear to be entirely independent.

It is necessary therefore to explain what is meant by aggregating *any* two ratios, i.e. two ratios whose terms are all independent.

*Def.* 28. THE PROCESS OF AGGREGATING RATIOS.

Let the ratios to be aggregated be $A : B$ and $C : D$.

Take any arbitrary magnitude $Z$.

Then find* two others $X$ and $Y$ such that

$$A : B = X : Z,$$
$$C : D = Y : Z.$$

Then
$$(A : B) \frown (C : D)$$
$$= (X : Z) \frown (Y : Z)$$
$$= X + Y : Z.$$

STAGE 4. The *form* of the resulting ratio found in the third stage depends on the value of the arbitrary magnitude $Z$. If the process is to be of any use it is necessary to show that the *value* of the resulting ratio does not depend on the *value* of $Z$.

This will be accomplished when it is shown that if any other magnitude be taken, say $Z'$, instead of $Z$, and the process repeated, then the value of the resulting ratio is unaltered.

Let therefore $X'$, $Y'$ be found so that

$$A : B = X' : Z',$$
$$C : D = Y' : Z'.$$

Then
$$(A : B) \frown (C : D)$$
$$= (X' : Z') \frown (Y' : Z')$$
$$= X' + Y' : Z'.$$

Since
$$A : B = X : Z,$$
and
$$A : B = X' : Z',$$
$$\therefore\ X : Z = X' : Z'.$$ [Prop. 10.

* This assumes the Fundamental Proposition in the Theory of Scales.

Since $C : D = Y : Z$,

and $C : D = Y' : Z'$,

$\therefore \; Y : Z = Y' : Z'$. [Prop. 10.

Since $X : Z = X' : Z'$,

and $Y : Z = Y' : Z'$,

$\therefore \; X + Y : Z = X' + Y' : Z'$. [Prop. 61.

i.e. the *value* of the resulting ratio is unaltered.

This is the justification of the process, and shows that it always leads to consistent results.

## Art. 192. EXAMPLES.

**111.** If the measure of $A : B$ be $\rho$,

and if the measure of $C : D$ be $\sigma$,

prove that $(A : B) \frown (C : D) = \rho + \sigma : 1$.

Hence show that the measure of the ratio aggregated from two ratios is the sum of the measures of those ratios.

**112.** (i) Prove that

$$(A : B) \frown (C : D) = (C : D) \frown (A : B).$$

(ii) Prove that $[(A : B) \frown (C : D)] \frown (E : F)$

$$= (A : B) \frown [(C : D) \frown (E : F)].$$

## Art. 193. ARITHMETICAL APPLICATION OF THE PROCESS OF AGGREGATING RATIOS.

If $r$, $s$, $u$, $v$ are integers, prove that

$$(r : s) \frown (u : v) = (vr + us : vs).$$

[This corresponds to the Arithmetical Theorem $\frac{r}{s} + \frac{u}{v} = \frac{vr + us}{vs}$.]

Now $r : s = vr : vs$ [Prop. 9.

and $u : v = us : vs$. [Prop. 9.

$$\therefore \; (r : s) \frown (u : v)$$
$$= (vr : vs) \frown (us : vs)$$
$$= vr + us : vs.$$

## Art. 194. EXAMPLE 113.

Prove that
$$[(A : B) \frown (C : D)] \divideontimes (E : F)$$
$$= [(A : B) \divideontimes (E : F)] \frown [(C : D) \divideontimes (E : F)].$$

## Art. 195. PROPOSITION LXII. (Euc. V. 4.)

ENUNCIATION 1. If two ratios are equal, and if equimultiples of the antecedents and equimultiples of the consequents be taken, then the multiple of the first antecedent has to that of its consequent the same ratio as the multiple of the second antecedent has to that of its consequent;

i.e. if $$A : B = X : Y,$$
to prove that $$rA : sB = rX : sY.$$

ENUNCIATION 2. *If the scale of* $A$, $B$ *is the same as that of* $X$, $Y$; *then the scale of* $rA$, $sB$ *is the same as that of* $rX$, $sY$.

*i.e. if* $$[A, B] \simeq [X, Y],$$
*then* $$[rA, sB] \simeq [rX, sY].$$

Take any integer $p$ in the first column,

and any integer $q$ in the second column,

of the scale of $rA$, $sB$.

There are three alternatives

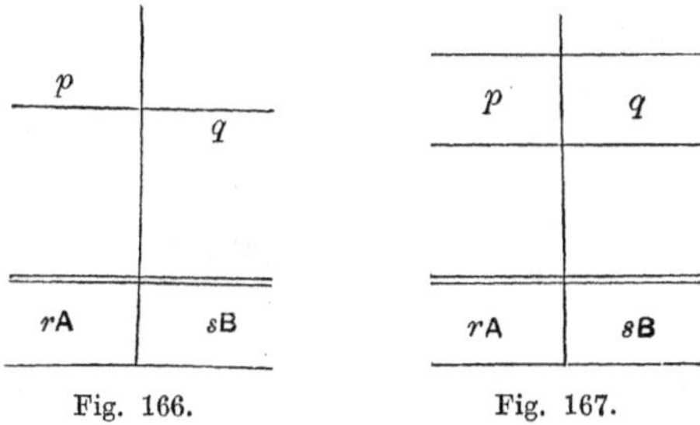


Fig. 166. Fig. 167.

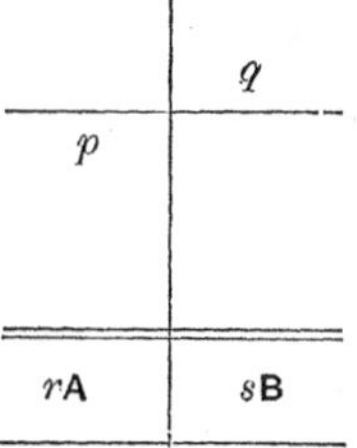


Fig. 168.

which express the facts

| | | | |
|---|---|---|---|
| | $p(rA) > q(sB)$ | $p(rA) = q(sB)$ | $p(rA) < q(sB)$ |
| i.e. | $prA > qsB$ | $prA = qsB$ | $prA < qsB.$ |

These correspond to the figures

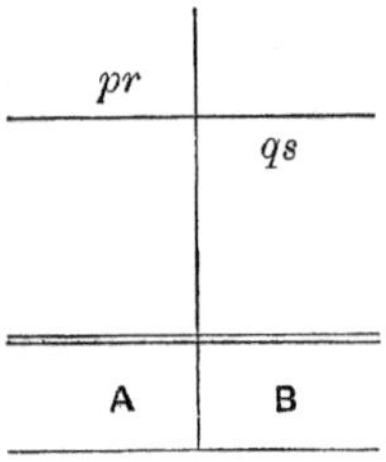

Fig. 169.

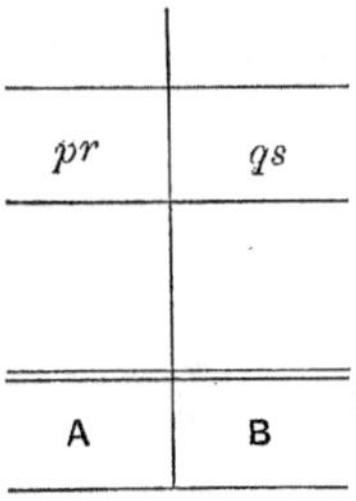

Fig. 170.

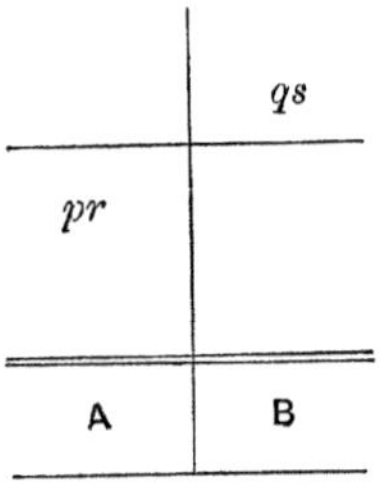

Fig. 171.

Now $$[A, B] \simeq [X, Y].$$

Hence there are the figures

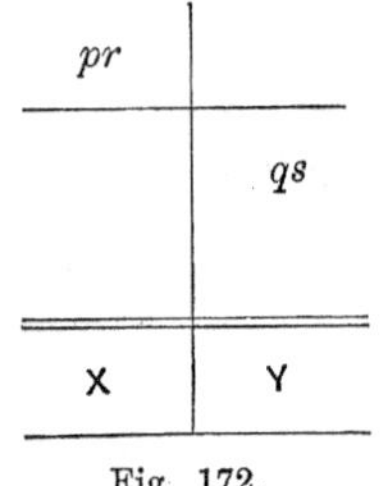

Fig. 172.

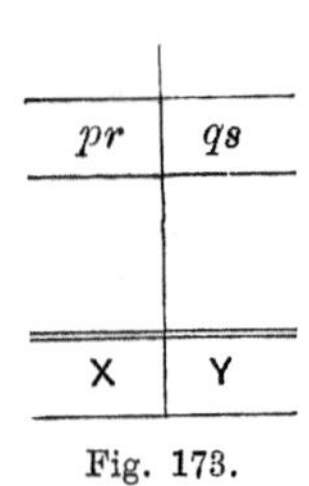

Fig. 173.

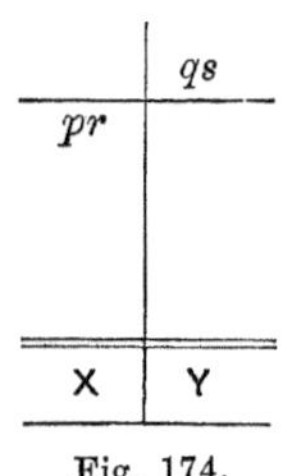

Fig. 174.

These express the facts

$$prX > qsY \qquad prX = qsY \qquad prX < qsY$$

i.e. $$p(rX) > q(sY) \qquad p(rX) = q(sY) \qquad p(rX) < q(sY).$$

Hence there are the figures

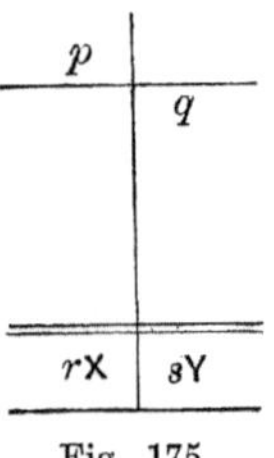

Fig. 175.

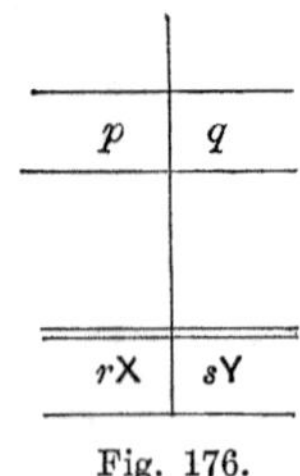

Fig. 176.

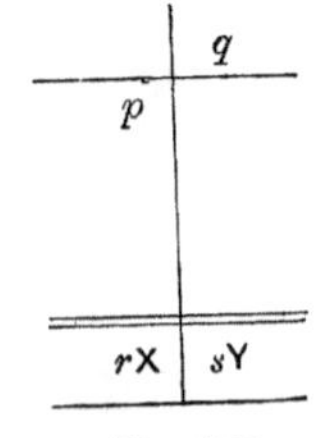

Fig. 177.

Comparing the Figures 166, 167, 168 with the Figures 175, 176, 177 respectively, it follows that

$$[rA, sB] \simeq [rX, sY].$$

### Art. 196. EXAMPLE 114.

Prove the converse of Proposition 62, viz.

If $$[rA, sB] \simeq [rX, sY],$$

then $$[A, B] \simeq [X, Y].$$

### Art. 197. PROPOSITION LXIII.

ENUNCIATION. *If $K$, $L$, $M$, $P$ be four straight lines in proportion, if the lengths of $L$ and $M$ be fixed, if the length of $K$ can be made smaller than that of any line however small, to show that the length of $P$ can be made greater than that of any line $Q$, however great $Q$ may be.*

By the Axiom of Art. 23, it is always possible to find an integer $r$ such that

$$rM > Q.$$

Now divide $L$ into $r$ equal parts, and take $K$ smaller than one of these equal parts.

Then $$rK < L.$$

Now $$K : L = M : P.$$

$$\therefore\ rK : L = rM : P. \qquad \text{[Prop. 62.}$$

Now $$rK < L.$$

$$\therefore\ rM < P. \qquad \text{[Art. 68.}$$

But $$Q < rM.$$

$$\therefore\ Q < P.$$

### Art. 198. EXAMPLE 115.

If $K$, $L$, $M$, $P$ be four straight lines in proportion, if the lengths of $L$, $M$ be fixed, and if the length of $K$ can be made greater than that of any line however great, show that the length of $P$ can be made smaller than that of any line $Q$ however small.

# SECTION XI.

## OTHER PROPOSITIONS IN THE THEORY OF SCALES AND OF RATIO.

Props. 64, 65.

### Art. 199. PROPOSITION LXIV. (Euc. V. 19.)

ENUNCIATION 1. If $A$, $B$, $C$, $D$ are magnitudes of the same kind, and

$$A : B = C : D,$$

prove that

$$A \sim C : B \sim D = A : B.$$

ENUNCIATION 2. *If $A$, $B$, $C$, $D$ are magnitudes of the same kind, and*

$$[A, B] \simeq [C, D],$$

*prove that*

$$[A \sim C, B \sim D] \simeq [A, B].$$

$$[A, B] \simeq [C, D].$$

$\therefore\ [A, C] \simeq [B, D].$ [Prop. 22.

$\therefore\ [A \sim C, C] \simeq [B \sim D, D].$ [Prop. 58.

$\therefore\ [A \sim C, B \sim D] \simeq [C, D].$ [Prop. 22.

$\therefore\ [A \sim C, B \sim D] \simeq [A, B].$ [Prop. 10.

### Art. 200. EXAMPLE 116.

If $X$, $A$, $S$, $A'$ are four harmonic points, $A$ and $A'$ being conjugate, and if $C$ be the middle point of $AA'$, prove that

$$SA : AX = CS : CA = CA : CX.$$

### Art. 201. PROPOSITION LXV. (Euc. V. 25.)

ENUNCIATION 1. If four magnitudes of the same kind are proportional, then the greatest and least of them together are greater than the sum of the other two.

ENUNCIATION 2. *If A, B, C, D are four magnitudes of the same kind, and if*

$$[A, B] \simeq [C, D],$$

*then the sum of the greatest and least is greater than the sum of the other two.*

Suppose $A$ the greatest.

Then $A > B$.

$\therefore\ C > D$. [Art. 68.

Again $\because\ [A, B] \simeq [C, D]$,

$\therefore\ [A, C] \simeq [B, D]$. [Prop. 22.

Now $A > C$.

$\therefore\ B > D$. [Art. 68.

Hence $D$ is the least of the four magnitudes.

Hence it is required to prove that

$$A + D > B + C.$$

Since $[A, B] \simeq [C, D]$,

$\therefore\ [A - B, B] \simeq [C - D, D]$. [Prop. 58.

$\therefore\ [A - B, C - D] \simeq [B, D]$. [Prop. 22.

Now $B > D$.

$\therefore\ A - B > C - D$. [Art. 68.

$\therefore\ A + D > B + C$.

### Art. 202. EXAMPLE 117.

If three quantities be in proportion, show that the sum of the extremes will exceed double the mean.

# NOTES.

**Art. 203.** NOTE 1. ON PROPS. 1—5, 6, 9, 11.

Props. 1—5 relate to certain simple cases of the application of the Commutative, Associative and Distributive Laws, with which the reader who has commenced elementary Algebra is already familiar.

Prop. I. $r(A+B) = rA + rB.$

Treating $A+B$ as the multiplicand,

and $r$ as the multiplier,

it is seen that the *multiplicand* is divided (or distributed) into its parts $A$, $B$.

Prop. II. $(a+b)R = aR + bR.$

Treating $a+b$ as the multiplier,

and $R$ as the multiplicand,

it is seen that the *multiplier* is distributed into its parts $a$, $b$.

Prop. III. If $A > B,$

$$r(A-B) = rA - rB.$$

Here the *multiplicand* $A-B$ is distributed into its parts $A$, $B$. !

Prop. IV. If $a > b,$

$$(a-b)R = aR - bR.$$

Here the *multiplier* $a-b$ is distributed into its parts $a$, $b$.

Prop. V. $r(sA) = (rs)A = (sr)A = s(rA).$

This illustrates both the Commutative and Associative Laws.

The fact $(rs)A = (sr)A$

illustrates the Commutative Law.

The fact that $r(sA) = (rs)A$

and the fact that $(sr)A = s(rA)$

both illustrate the Associative Law.

If Propositions 1—4, 6, 9, 11 be arranged in parallel columns, thus:—

I. $r(A+B)=rA+rB.$ II. $(a+b)R=aR+bR.$

III. $r(A-B)=rA-rB.$ IV. $(a-b)R=aR-bR.$

VI (i). If $A \gtreqless B,$ VI (iii). If $a \gtreqless b,$

then $rA \gtreqless rB.$ then $aR \gtreqless bR.$

VI (ii). If $rA \gtreqless rB,$ VI (iv). If $aR \gtreqless bR,$

then $A \gtreqless B.$ then $a \gtreqless b.$

IX. $[A, B] \simeq [nA, nB].$ XI. $[a, b] \simeq [aN, bN].$

then the two propositions in any one line are related to each other in such a manner that magnitudes in either are replaced by whole numbers in the other.

### Art. 204. NOTE 2. On Prop. 5.

The following proposition is deducible from Prop. 5.

### PROPOSITION LXVI.

Enunciation. *If the magnitudes $A$ and $rA$ be each divided into $s$ equal parts, prove that any one of the parts into which $rA$ is divided will be $r$ times as great as any one of the parts into which $A$ is divided.*

Suppose that each of the parts into which $A$ is divided is $B$.

Then $$A=sB.$$

$$\therefore\ rA=rsB=s(rB). \qquad \text{[Prop. 5.}$$

Hence each of the $s$ equal parts into which $rA$ is divided is $rB$, which is $r$ times as great as each of the $s$ equal parts into which $A$ is divided.

If then $\dfrac{A}{s}$ denote the $s$th part of $A$,

$\dfrac{rA}{s}$ will denote the $s$th part of $rA$,

and this proposition may be expressed thus:—

$$\frac{rA}{s}=rB=r\left(\frac{A}{s}\right).$$

$$\therefore\ \frac{rA}{s}=r\left(\frac{A}{s}\right).$$

### Art. 205. NOTE 3. ON PROP. 9.

The following proposition is deducible from Prop. 9.

### PROPOSITION LXVII.

ENUNCIATION. *To prove that*

$$[A, B] \simeq \left[\frac{rA}{n}, \frac{rB}{n}\right].$$

Since $[C, D] \simeq [nC, nD]$ [Prop. 9.

and $[C, D] \simeq [rC, rD]$, [Prop. 9.

$\therefore\ [nC, nD] \simeq [rC, rD]$. [Prop. 10.

Put

$$nC = A,$$

$$nD = B.$$

$$\therefore\ C = \frac{A}{n},$$

$$D = \frac{B}{n},$$

$$rC = r\left(\frac{A}{n}\right) = \frac{rA}{n},$$ [Prop. 66.

$$rD = r\left(\frac{B}{n}\right) = \frac{rB}{n}.$$ [Prop. 66.

$$\therefore\ [A, B] \simeq \left[\frac{rA}{n}, \frac{rB}{n}\right].$$

### Art. 206. NOTE 4. ON PROP. 12.

The twelfth proposition deals with differing relative multiple scales, upon which the theory of unequal ratios depends. It leads naturally to the criterion for distinguishing the greater of two unequal ratios from the smaller thus:—

Taking as a fundamental idea that if $A$ be greater than $E$, then the ratio of $A$ to $B$ is greater than the ratio of $E$ to $B$.

Then changing in Prop. 12, $B$ into $E$ and $C$ into $B$ it follows that integers $r$, $n$ exist such that

$$rA > nB,$$

but

$$rE < nB.$$

Now let $D$ be any magnitude, and let $C$ be any other magnitude of the same kind as $D$ such that

$$[E, B] \simeq [C, D],^*$$

or in Euclid's language $$E : B = C : D.$$

Since $$rE < nB,$$

$$\therefore\ rC < nD.$$

Consequently $$A : B > C : D,$$

and integers $r$, $n$ exist such that

$$rA > nB,$$

but $$rC < nD.$$

These are equivalent to, but not quite the same in form as, the conditions which Euclid gives in the 7th Definition of the 5th Book as the conditions to be satisfied in order that $A : B$ may be greater than $C : D$.

Euclid's form of the criterion may be obtained by proceeding thus:—

Taking as fundamental ideas

(I) If $X$, $Y$, $Z$ be magnitudes of the same kind, then

($\alpha$) if $X : Z$ is greater than $Y : Z$,

then $X$ is greater than $Y$.

($\beta$) if $X : Z$ is not greater than $Y : Z$,

then $X$ is not greater than $Y$.

(II) If the ratio $A : B$ is greater than the ratio $C : D$, then there exists a ratio, say $n : r$, of some two whole numbers, such that

$A : B$ is greater than $n : r$,

but $C : D$ is not greater than $n : r$.

Then it is possible to proceed thus:—

Since $$A : B = rA : rB,$$ [Prop. 9.

and $$n : r = nB : rB,$$ [Prop. 11.

then the assertion that

$A : B$ is greater than $n : r$,

may be expressed in the form that

$rA : rB$ is greater than $nB : rB$,

* This assumes the Fundamental Proposition in the Theory of Scales.

and hence by I ($\alpha$) involves the fact that

$$rA \text{ is greater than } nB.$$

Again $C : D = rC : rD,$ [Prop. 9.

and $n : r = nD : rD.$ [Prop. 11.

Therefore the assertion that

$$C : D \text{ is not greater than } n : r,$$

may be expressed in the form that

$$rC : rD \text{ is not greater than } nD : rD,$$

and therefore by I ($\beta$) involves the fact that

$$rC \text{ is not greater than } nD.$$

Hence if $A : B$ is greater than $C : D$, then some integers $n$, $r$ exist such that

$$rA \text{ is greater than } nB,$$

whilst $rC$ is not greater than $nD$.

This is the 7th Definition of the Fifth Book of Euclid.

## Art. 207. NOTE 5. On the Definition of Ratio. (Art. 62.)

Euclid's Definition of Ratio (the third Definition of the Fifth Book) is as follows:

Λόγος ἐστὶ δύο μεγεθῶν ὁμογενῶν ἡ κατὰ πηλικότητα πρὸς ἄλληλα ποιὰ σχέσις.

De Morgan translates it thus:

"Ratio is a certain mutual habitude of two magnitudes of the same kind depending on their quantuplicity."

The word "quantuplicity" which represents the Greek "πηλικότης" is especially difficult. It contains the idea of relative magnitude.

De Morgan defines Ratio as Relative Magnitude on page 63 of his *Treatise on the Connexion of Number and Magnitude.*

### Art. 208. NOTE 6. On Prop. 22.

In order to complete the proof of Prop. 22 without using Prop. 8 (ii) it is necessary to show directly that

if $[A, B] \simeq [C, D]$,

and if $rA = sC$, then $rB = sD$.

If $rA = sC$,

then $[rA, B] \simeq [sC, B]$. [Prop. 20.

Now $[A, B] \simeq [C, D]$,

$\therefore\ [rA, B] \simeq [rC, D]$. [Prop. 62.

$\therefore\ [sC, B] \simeq [rC, D]$. [Prop. 10.

The required result follows from this by so altering the terms of the scales that the 1st term is the same in each.

Now $[sC, B] \simeq [rsC, rB]$ [Prop. 9.

and $[rC, D] \simeq [srC, sD] \simeq [rsC, sD]$. [Prop. 9.

$\therefore\ [rsC, rB] \simeq [rsC, sD]$.

$\therefore\ rB = sD$. [Prop. 21.

ANOTHER PROOF.

Since $[A, B] \simeq [C, D]$,

$\because\ [rA, rB] \simeq [A, B]$, [Prop. 9.

and $[sC, sD] \simeq [C, D]$, [Prop. 9.

$\therefore\ [rA, rB] \simeq [sC, sD]$. [Prop. 10.

But $rA = sC$,

$\therefore\ rB = sD$. [Prop. 21.

### Art. 209. NOTE 7. On Prop. 24.

The 24th Proposition is a very suggestive one. It not only leads naturally to the consideration of the point at infinity on a straight line, which is briefly treated below, but also to the consideration of negative ratios (which are not treated in this book).

It has been shown that if $K : L$ is not a ratio of equality, then there is one way of dividing $AB$ internally and one way of dividing it externally in the ratio $K : L$.

Let the internal point of division be $C$, and the external point of division $C'$, then it appears from the figures of Prop. 24 that $C$ and $C'$ always lie on the same side of the middle point of $AB$.

Further it follows from Prop. 60 that

$$\text{the rect. } OC \,.\, OC' = \text{the square on } OA.$$

Now suppose that the length of $K$ is fixed, and let the effect of diminishing the length of $L$ down to equality with that of $K$ be investigated.

Then $AC$ and $CB$ tend to become equal, and therefore $C$ approaches $O$, and by making the difference of $K$ and $L$ sufficiently small the length $OC$ may be made smaller than any length however small; and therefore by Prop. 63 the length of $OC'$ can be made greater than any length however great.

Similar conclusions can be drawn from the case in which $K$ is greater than $L$, except that $C$ and $C'$ are on the same side of $O$ as $B$.

When however $K = L$, the internal point of division is the middle point, but the external point of division does not exist from Euclid's point of view; because Euclid regards parallel straight lines as never meeting and so the construction fails in this case.

Hence from Euclid's point of view it is impossible to state generally that to every point $C$ on $AB$ between $A$ and $B$ there corresponds a point $C'$ such that $C''$ divides $AB$ externally in the same ratio as $C$ divides $AB$, because there is no point corresponding to the middle point of $AB$.

From the point of view of Modern Geometry in which a straight line is supposed to have *one* point at infinity, when $C$ is at the middle point of $AB$, $C'$ is at infinity; and the theorem can be stated quite generally that there is one way of dividing $AB$ internally and one way of dividing it externally in *any* given ratio $K : L$.

## Art. 210. NOTE 8. ON ART. 106.

The contents of Art. 106 may perhaps be more easily appreciated by considering the following numerical case.

Consider the triangle whose sides are $a$, $b$, $c$; and the triangle whose sides are $\frac{k^2}{a}$, $\frac{k^2}{b}$, $\frac{k^2}{c}$.

Then
$$b : c = \frac{k^2}{c} : \frac{k^2}{b};$$
$$c : a = \frac{k^2}{a} : \frac{k^2}{c};$$
$$a : b = \frac{k^2}{b} : \frac{k^2}{a};$$

so that any two sides of one triangle are proportional to some two sides of the other.

But the two triangles do not satisfy the condition in the enunciation of Prop. 27 implied in the words "taken in order."

E.g. whilst $b$ corresponds to $\frac{k^2}{c}$ in the 1st proportion,

it corresponds to $\frac{k^2}{a}$ in the 3rd proportion.

As a numerical example take $a = 5$, $b = 3$, $c = 4$ and $k^2 = 60$.

Then $\frac{k^2}{a} = 12$, $\frac{k^2}{b} = 20$, $\frac{k^2}{c} = 15$;

and we have
$$3 : 4 = 15 : 20$$
$$4 : 5 = 12 : 15$$
$$3 : 5 = 12 : 20.$$

But since
$$5^2 = 3^2 + 4^2,$$
but
$$(20)^2 \neq (12)^2 + (15)^2;$$
the first triangle is right-angled, the second is not; and therefore the triangles are not similar.

### Art. 211. NOTE 9. On Prop. 35.

In order to complete the proof of Prop. 35 without using Prop. 8 (ii) it is necessary to show directly that

if
$$[A, B] \simeq [T, U],$$
if
$$[B, C] \simeq [U, V],$$
and if $rA = sC$, then $rT = sV$.

If
$$rA = sC,$$
then
$$[rA, B] \simeq [sC, B]. \quad \text{[Prop. 20.}$$
Since
$$[A, B] \simeq [T, U],$$
$$\therefore [rA, B] \simeq [rT, U]. \quad \text{[Prop. 62.}$$
Since
$$[B, C] \simeq [U, V],$$
$$\therefore [B, sC] \simeq [U, sV]. \quad \text{[Prop. 62.}$$
$$\therefore [sC, B] \simeq [sV, U]. \quad \text{[Prop. 19.}$$
$$\therefore [rT, U] \simeq [sV, U]. \quad \text{[Prop. 10.}$$
$$\therefore rT = sV. \quad \text{[Prop. 21.}$$

$\therefore$ if $rA = sC$, then $rT = sV$.

**Art. 212.** NOTE 10. COROLLARY TO PROP. 42.

The following proof of this Corollary does not depend on the properties of duplicate ratio.

*The areas of similar triangles are proportional to the areas of the squares described on corresponding sides.*

Let $ABC$, $DEF$ be similar triangles.

Let $AB$, $DE$ be corresponding sides.

On $AB$, $DE$ describe the squares $ABLK$, $DENM$.

It is required to prove that

$$\triangle ABC : \triangle DEF = \text{square } ABLK : \text{square } DENM.$$

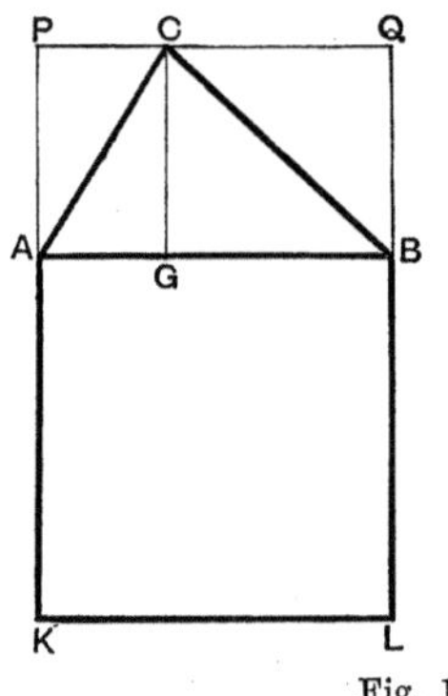


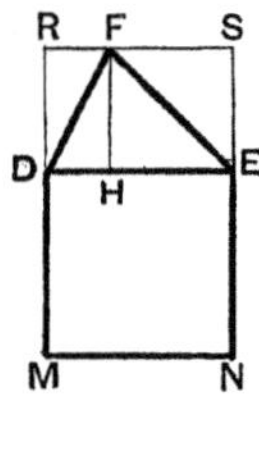


Fig. 178.

Draw $CG$ perpendicular to $AB$, and $FH$ perpendicular to $DE$.

Describe on $AB$ the rectangle $ABQP$ having the same altitude as the triangle $ABC$, and on $DE$ the rectangle $DESR$ having the same altitude as the triangle $DEF$.

The triangles $ACG$, $DFH$ are similar, for

$$C\hat{A}G = F\hat{D}H,$$

$$C\hat{G}A = F\hat{H}D,$$

$$\therefore\ A\hat{C}G = D\hat{F}H.$$

Hence the triangles are similar by Prop. 26.

$\therefore\ CG : CA = FH : FD,$

$\therefore\ CG : FH = CA : FD,$ [Prop. 22.

but $CA : FD = AB : DE,$

since the triangles are similar;

$\therefore\ CG : FH = AB : DE,$ [Prop. 10.

i.e. $AP : DR = AK : DM,$

$\therefore\ AP : AK = DR : DM,$ [Prop. 22.

$\therefore$ rect. $ABQP$ : square $ABLK$ = rect. $DESR$ : square $DENM$,

$\therefore$ rect. $ABQP$ : rect. $DESR$ = square $ABLK$ : square $DENM$. [Prop. 22.

Now rect. $ABQP = 2\triangle ABC$

and rect. $DESR = 2\triangle DEF,$

$\therefore$ rect. $ABQP$ : rect. $DESR = \triangle ABC : \triangle DEF,$ [Art. 42.

$\therefore\ \triangle ABC : \triangle DEF$ = square $ABLK$ : square $DENM$.

### Art. 213. NOTE 11. On Prop. 56.

($\alpha$) In order to complete the proof of Prop. 56 without using Prop. 8 (ii) it is necessary to prove directly that

if $[A, B] \simeq [U, V],$

if $[B, C] \simeq [T, U],$

and if $rA = sC$, then $rT = sV$.

If $rA = sC,$

then $[rA, B] \simeq [sC, B]$ .................. (I). [Prop. 20.

Now $[A, B] \simeq [U, V],$

$\therefore\ [rA, B] \simeq [rU, V]$ .............. (II). [Prop. 62.

Further $[B, C] \simeq [T, U],$

$\therefore\ [C, B] \simeq [U, T],$ [Prop. 19.

$\therefore\ [sC, B] \simeq [sU, T]$ ............... (III). [Prop. 62.

From (I), (II), (III) by Prop. 10 it follows that

$[rU, V] \simeq [sU, T]$ ............... (IV).

In the last result it is possible to transform the terms of the scales so that the first element is the same in each.

$[rU, V] \simeq [srU, sV]$...............(V), [Prop. 9.

$[sU, T] \simeq [rsU, rT]$ ........... (VI). [Prop. 9.

From (IV), (V), (VI) by Prop. 10 it follows that

$$[srU, sV] \simeq [rsU, rT].$$

But $$srU = rsU,$$

$$\therefore\ sV = rT. \qquad \text{[Prop. 21.}$$

$\therefore$ if $rA = sC$, then $rT = sV$.

($\beta$) Propositions 35 and 56 are so nearly alike in form that the difference between them should be carefully noted.

Arranging them in parallel columns:—

| | Prop. 35. | | Prop. 56. |
|---|---|---|---|
| If | $[A, B] \simeq [T, U]$, | If | $[A, B] \simeq [U, V]$, |
| and if | $[B, C] \simeq [U, V]$, | and if | $[B, C] \simeq [T, U]$, |
| then | $[A, C] \simeq [T, V]$. | then | $[A, C] \simeq [T, V]$. |

it appears that the positions of the scales $[T, U]$, $[U, V]$ in Prop. 35 are interchanged in Prop. 56.

## Art. 214. NOTE 12. On Prop. 58.

The statement on lines 3—5 of Page 118 *that two scales in which the first term is zero may be considered to be the same* may present some difficulty, inasmuch as a relative multiple scale presupposes the existence of two magnitudes, and the relative multiple scale of zero and a magnitude has not been defined.

Without going fully into the subject, which here touches upon the difficulties of the Infinitesimal Calculus, it may be sufficient to remark that since

$$\left[\frac{A}{n}, A\right] \simeq \left[A, nA\right], \qquad \text{[Prop. 9.}$$

and $$\because\ [A, nA] \simeq [1, n], \qquad \text{[Prop. 11.}$$

and $$\because\ \left[1, n\right] \simeq \left[\frac{1}{n}, 1\right], \qquad \text{[Art. 44.}$$

$$\therefore\ \left[\frac{A}{n}, A\right] \simeq \left[\frac{1}{n}, 1\right]. \qquad \text{[Prop. 10.}$$

Hence the measure of the ratio of $\frac{A}{n}$ to $A$ is the rational fraction $\frac{1}{n}$.

Now imagine the integer $n$ to increase without limit, then $\frac{A}{n}$ tends to the limit zero, and therefore the scale of $\frac{A}{n}$, $A$ is one in which the first term tends to the limit zero, whilst at the same time the measure, viz. $\frac{1}{n}$, of the ratio of the two terms of the scale tends to the limit zero.

Now when the terms of a scale are given, they determine a ratio, and also its measure.

Conversely, when the measure of a ratio is given, the corresponding scale is determined.

If then the measure of a certain ratio is zero, it is possible to say either that there is no corresponding scale, or that there is one and only one corresponding scale. The latter alternative is the one implied in the text.

In this connection the following proposition is of interest.

*If the scale of $A$, $B$ is the same as that of $C$, $D$; if $A$ can be made as small as we please, and if $B$ and $D$ be fixed magnitudes, then $C$ can be made smaller than any magnitude $E$, however small $E$ may be.*

It is possible by Archimedes' Axiom to choose $n$ so that

$$nE > D;$$

and by hypothesis $A$ can be taken smaller than $\frac{B}{n}$,

i.e. $$nA < B.$$

But $$[A, B] \simeq [C, D].$$

$$\therefore\ nC < D.$$

$$\therefore\ nC < nE.$$

$$\therefore\ C < E.$$

So that when the first term of the scale of $A$, $B$ tends to zero, so also does the first term of the scale of $C$, $D$.

Another proposition of a similar kind is this:—

*If the scale of $A$, $B$ is the same as that of $C$, $D$; if $A$ can be made as small as we please, if $C$ and $D$ be fixed magnitudes, then $B$ can be made smaller than any magnitude $E$, however small $E$ may be.*

It is possible by Archimedes' Axiom to choose $n$ so that

$$nC > D.$$

Then since $$[A, B] \simeq [C, D]$$

$$\therefore \ nA > B.$$

Now by hypothesis $A$ can be made as small as we please.

Choose therefore

$$A < \frac{E}{n},$$

i.e. $$nA < E.$$

$$\therefore \ B < E.$$

Hence if the scale of $A$, $B$ be given, and one term tend to zero, so does the other.

# INDEX.

*The references are to the Articles.*

CAMBRIDGE: PRINTED BY J. AND C. F. CLAY, AT THE UNIVERSITY PRESS.

www.ingramcontent.com/pod-product-compliance
Lightning Source LLC
LaVergne TN
LVHW010608110826
845149LV00003B/823

*9781418179991*